STOP WASTING YOUR MONEY

. . . And Pay for Your Holiday Instead

Conor Pope

D1151824

LIB
ERT
I ES

To Nina

Contents

STOP WASTING YOUR MONEY

Introduction

This is not the ultimate penny pincher's guide to thrifty living. If that's what you're looking for, you'll be glad to know that there are already dozens of such books on the market, filled with thousands of 'money-saving tips' which, if followed religiously, will see your annual spend fall dramatically.

In front of me now, I have *Mr Thrifty's How to Save Money on Absolutely Everything*, *Thrifty Ways for Modern Days* and *The Penny Pincher's Book Revisited* – so good they wrote it twice.

Mr Thrifty tells me that I should make contact with contact-lens research labs and volunteer to test their products in clinical settings – and in so doing save myself a fortune when it comes to actually buying lenses. Anxious to turn me into a medical experiment, Mr Thrifty also thinks that it would be a fine

idea to have my teeth seen to for free by trainee dentists in a nearby dental hospital (presuming there is one nearby) and to get in touch with drug manufacturers to see if they're trialling any products I might find useful for treating any ailments I may have – like the stress-related ulcer caused by the endless worrying about my new role as a human guinea pig and the sudden-onset blindness brought on by faulty contact lenses, perhaps. On top of that, he thinks it's a good idea to make friends with a pilot for jaunts abroad and to wear flip-flops all year round to save on the wearing and washing of socks. Mr Thrifty is quite clearly bonkers.

Then there are the Penny Pinchers, a lovely couple in their late sixties whom I spoke to for a feature in the *Irish Times*

recently. They are not mean at all, the nice lady told me repeatedly, it's just that they never spend any money on anything unless they absolutely have to. No store-bought treats ever darken their doors, no designer labels are ever worn, and no holidays or weekends away in posh hotels are ever taken – although they do like to drive for a few days in one direction in their battered old car before turning round and driving home again. Fun times!

The Penny Pinchers tell me that a dead bird swinging silently from a tree at the back of my garden will serve as an excellent – and free – bird-scarer. They don't tell me why I might want to scare birds, or where I get my dead bird, or what happens if a cat eats my dead bird, or what I am supposed to use to scare the cats off? A dead cat, presumably, and before you know it I'll have become a latter-day old lady who swallowed a fly. The Penny

Pinchers also suggest that I keep my tights (how did they know?) and candles in the fridge to stop them laddering and burning too quickly, and use egg white as glue and beeswax as a cheap chewing-gum replacement. The Penny Pinchers are quite clearly bonkers. Lovely, but bonkers.

Thrifty Ways, meanwhile, is edited by Martin Lewis, a serious-minded British journalist who always has money on his mind. This particular book – which, I should point out, is unlike most of his serious-minded journalism – is made up of homespun tips and tricks posted by readers of his website. This has culminated in page after page of headache-inducing ways for me to clean and fix my house for nothing, feed my family for peanuts, and dress for buttons.

This is not that sort of book. This book is much simpler.

When, in her role as enterprise minister, Mary Harney

STOP WASTING YOUR MONEY

once suggested that all consumers needed to do to avoid paying high prices was to shop around for bargains, critics rounded on her as some latter-day Marie Antoinette who was completely out of touch with the grim rip-off reality her subjects faced daily.

Just as the French peasants had no cake to eat, Irish consumers had precious little choice when it came to the sky-high prices they had to pay for everything from a pint to a kilowatt of electricity, her critics said. And they were right: Harney's glib comment completely failed to address the problem of rising prices in Ireland.

To be fair to her, she may have had a point, even if she made it sound Idiotically simplistic. Even when every retailer is charging over the odds for everything and when all the restaurants, pubs, insurance companies, mobile-phone operators and utilities

seem focused on wringing every last cent from each of us each and every month, there are still ways we can fight back – and sometimes it *does* actually involve shopping around.

On other occasions, it involves not shopping at all, and giving a resolute two fingers to the rip-off merchants who screw us just because they can.

This book is not intended to be hectoring or judgemental – that's what Eddie Hobbs is for – but rather it sets out to illustrate that, by thinking about the money you're spending and swapping some bad habits for good ones, you can save yourself the price of a holiday somewhere sunny or snowy each and every year.

And it doesn't have to be hard. Let's say you decided that, for three days a week for the rest of the year, you'd make your own sandwiches and bring them to work instead of forking out a fiver for some sweaty bread and a sorry-looking filling. Not only would this be better for your wallet (to the tune of at least €300 a year), it would also be better for your health (as long as it's not calorific breakfast rolls you're bringing into work with you), and it'll taste better too.

Then there's something as inherently dull as insurance – be it motor, house or health. By shopping round – though not in a literal, pounding-the-streets sense (that's what phones and the Internet are for) – hundreds if not thousands of euro can be saved each year.

Shopping online instead of in the high street will also save you a considerable amount of cash each year, and being wise to how much your bank and credit-card company is charging you can knock another few quid off your monthly outgoings. Then there are all those free phone calls, and free TV, out there just waiting for you to take advantage of them. The idea is that by

taking just a few small steps each month, you'll save yourself a couple of grand each year – which you can then blow, guilt-free, on your summer holidays.

Rather than attempting to introduce every possible money-saving idea you find here over the course of what would become a busy afternoon, it might be worthwhile adopting a gentler, baby-step approach to it and introducing some of the changes over the course of the next year, taking twelve steps to financial well-being.

By total coincidence, as well as there being twelve steps in my money-saving 'programme', there are twelve months in the year. Start saving money in Month 1 (whichever month of the year that is for you), and work your way through to the end of the year. By the end of the twelve months, the tenner you've just shelled out for this book will have saved you more than €1,000 – not only this year, but every year. And all without you losing the will to live along the way because your life has become monochrome and devoid of treats.

And there won't be a dead bird in sight, I promise.

Month 1

Watch it

It's New Year's Day, and you're hung over, your tongue is a little furry, and you're completely skint. Even if you haven't been on a three-week bender like the rest of the country, you've almost certainly eaten more than is good for you, and have probably developed party fatigue. At the beginning of his epic poem The Waste Land, T. S. Eliot claimed that April was the cruelest month; he was, of course, lying. January is the longest and the cruelest month of the year: nothing really happens, and nobody can afford to do anything. The only thing for it is to stay at home, counting the days till pay day and watching

the telly, because at least that's cheap, right? Of course it's not.

Watching television in Ireland can be a costly business. A twenty-five-year-old who takes out an annual TV subscription with one of the main providers (and there are only really two of them at present) and diligently buys a TV licence (€160 and rising) every year can expect to shell out in excess of €35,000 over the course of their lifetime. This is a lot of cash by any definition, but it is cash you don't have to spend at all: the same twenty-five-year-old can, by taking advantage of all the free television signals swirling about the place, pay a little less than €10,000 over the same long life – and most of that is on the licences.

More than one million Irish households seem content to fork out an average of €400 a year for their viewing pleasure. Two companies have the Irish market sewn up. UPC – which married the one-time rivals NTL and Chorus – and Sky TV. UPC has around 600,000 subscribers, while Sky has close to half a million digital subscribers in Ireland.

The prices both companies charge are broadly similar. (Fancy that!) Sky's charges start at €21.50 per month for an entry-level package and climb to €66 for the bells-and-whistles deal, which includes Sky Sports and multiple movie channels. Upgrading to Sky Plus – which allows users to pause live television and record programmes on to a set-top box – will cost an additional €149, plus an installation charge of €45, although it seems inevitable that Sky will drop that charge in order to build its subscriber base. High Definition service, meanwhile, costs an even less palatable €449 – and is it worth it? Absolutely not, at least not yet, given how few programmes are being made in high definition.

For its part, UPC is offering TV deals which start at €9.99 a month, a figure which sounds great until you realise that it's a promo offer which rises to over €20 a month after the first three months. The company's analogue package offers a very basic set-up for €21.49 a month, while the entry-level digital TV offering is €25.99.

With prices like these, it's a wonder that more people don't take advantage of the freeview satellite services that are legally available throughout the country at a fraction of the cost. There are a couple of approaches to take: the hard-core do-it-yourself option or the lazier get-someone-else-to-do-it-for-you option.

A satellite dish giving you access to more than two hundred channels – many of which are actually worth watching – can be bought for not much more than €100 in Lidl (although not all the time), while Maplin is selling kits which, it says, are idiot-proof, for around €120. One reader of 'Pricewatch' in the *Irish Times* recently got in touch to say how easy to assemble these kits are. He simply attached the dish to a tree at the back of his house and laid the cable in a trench he had dug through the garden. He now has lifetime access to more than 200 channels for less than a third of the cost of a Sky subscription for one year.

If all the digging, cable-laying and tree-climbing sounds too much like hard work – and, let's face it, it does – there is an easier way to get low-cost satellite television. There are dozens of satellite companies who will do it for you. Typically, companies offer installations for a one-off fee of €299. The service gives access to hundreds of stations, including all the BBC channels, ITV, Film Four, a range of children's channels, multiple news channels (including Sky News and CNN) and a host of other channels which are, in truth, of marginal interest.

The Irish channels are unavailable via free-to-air satellite, as they are contracted to Sky TV, although they can be accessed via a normal TV aerial. If you're wondering where the catch is, there is none – well, not really. If you go down this route, there is no customer support (although this might not displease anyone who has spent hours getting no satisfaction at all from NTL). There is also no guarantee of service, so, in the admittedly unlikely event that the BBC or ITV pull their free-to-air satellite service, those with dishes might be left with no option but to brush up on their German or go back, tail between their legs, to the traditional providers.

Saving: €100 in year one, and then €400 annually

STOP WASTING YOUR MONEY

Watch less, read more

Paying for a TV subscription costs money, but even the very act of watching it can prove to be a financial drain. Ads relentlessly encourage you to buy products which you don't want or need – and remember, if a product is advertised on the telly, it adds a significant percentage to the retail price, because it is not the manufacturer but you the shopper who will end up paying for it. It is not only the ads which are pushing products down your throat but the increasing prevalence of product placement. The only real solution is to watch less TV and maybe spend more time reading books, where product placement is not commonplace. At least not yet.

Just some of the channels available on free-to-air satellite service

National broadcasters: BBC 1, 2, 3 and 4 (all regions); ITV 1, 2, 3 and 4 (all regions); S4C; Channel 4 is joining in spring 2008

Movies: Film Four, True Movies, Movies4Men, Zone Horror, Zone Thriller

Kids' channels: CITV, CBBC, CBeebies

News channels: Sky News, BBC News 24, CNN, EuroNews

Sports: Extreme Sports

Music stations: Chartshow TV, Classic FM TV, Classics TV, Performance TV

Entertainment: Reality TV, Fashion TV, Motors TV

Radio stations: RTÉ, BBC and many more

Other channels: TV, PCNE (Chinese), The God Channel, EWTN

Gym'll fix it?

Unless you actively enjoy wasting money, you should never, ever join a gym in January. Of course, it seems very tempting. You're bloated and bored, and RTÉ has blown its budget on the blockbuster Christmas movies you saw three years ago in the cinema, so there's nothing on the telly. Even if you have 200 digital channels to flick through, it's all re-runs of Only Fools and Horses and weird, poorly lit programmes in which poorly paid presenters claim to be communicating with ghosts for the enjoyment of no one but a few easily fooled oddballs.

So your thoughts turn elsewhere. If the lifestyle pages of all the newspapers are to be believed, the whole world seems to be making resolutions to live cleaner, healthier lives – so why not join them? Because there is no worse time to join a gym then at the beginning of the year. Almost two-thirds of the people

who join a gym in January will have pretty much given up on it by St Patrick's Day. Yet most, having signed up for annual membership – or, worse still, paid their year's sub in full – continue to pay monthly subscriptions for a service they use infrequently at best.

Gyms are notoriously reluctant to discuss their charges over the phone, preferring instead to leave the grubby issue of money until they have given you a personal tour of their premises, so that they can better push the benefits of membership to you. But let's say that the average monthly cost of gym membership is €50 – in big urban centres it will almost certainly be more than that, annual membership will set you back €600.

People often delude themselves into thinking that spending a huge amount on gym membership will force them to go. It won't. All the experts recommend that New Year fitness optimists wait until February at the very earliest before taking the plunge. And before you do that, allocate three separate hours each week for several weeks beforehand for taking exercise – walking, cycling, skipping like a mad thing in your back garden. If you can't manage to put that time aside, then you might want to think long and hard about joining the gym.

If you are already a gym member, now might be a good time to carry out an audit of your usage (a fancy way of saying that you should be honest with yourself about how much you actually go, as opposed to how often you mean to go). If you find yourself bathed in sweat and gasping for breath on the cross trainer three times a week every week, then the €50 it's costing you a month is money well spent. If you only trouble the fancy machinery once a week – or less – cancel your membership immediately.

If you do decide to join a gym, make sure to read the terms and conditions carefully before you sign the forms: ridiculous clauses absolving the fitness centre of all liability in all circumstances are not uncommon. Many gyms don't make their minimum notice periods for contract cancellation clear, while others automatically roll over annual contracts. Many operators have no refund clauses in place, even when the operator breaks the terms of the contract, and summary cancellation of membership without cause or refund is an all-too-frequent occurrence.

Savings: At least €50

Die, detox diets, die!

Let's not beat about the bush here, detox diets and programmes are a complete waste of money, and the best financial resolution you could make would be not to waste any of yours on any of them. Not now, not ever.

Typically, a five-day 'detox' programme will cost around €20 in your local Boots, while the programmes available from health stores will inevitably cost more – although they do come in fancier boxes. They all promise to flush out your liver, get your digestive system back on track, replace the bad with the good and made you feel years younger, almost as if you hadn't spent your late teens and twenties downing vodka and Red Bull, smoking rollies and living off a diet of Abrakebabras and Jaffa Cakes.

The detox boxes are lying to you. They have no restorative powers and no medical or scientific basis. Talk to any doctor with an interest in such things, and they will confirm this. If you lay off the booze, the coffee and the smokes for the month, exercise just a little bit, and drink plenty of water (tap water, not overpriced mineral water, that's another con), you'll feel just as good, if not better, without having to spend a cent.

Saving: €30

A trimmer you

And while you're giving up the detox diets, you might want to consider knocking the faddy ones on the head too. While shedding a few pounds offers enormous benefits for people who are overweight, those benefits evaporate if the weight loss is done in the wrong way. The diet industry is one of the few industries that flourishes on failure, and if any of the diets to be found wedged on to shelves in our bookshops and shouting at us from the newsstands actually worked in the long term, it would spell the end of an industry which is worth billions of euro each year.

The Happy Diet, the Eat-all-day Diet, the Three-hour Diet (that sounds pretty simple!) are just three of at least a dozen new weight-loss programmes the glossy magazines in my local newsagents recently promised would lead to a thinner, happier me within weeks. Without actually opening any of these magazines, it's safe to assume that the diets carried within them will never actually deliver a leaner me. Quite apart from the fact that any programme calling itself the Eat-all-day diet seems doomed to failure, survey after survey has shown that between 90 and 95 percent of diets are unsuccessful.

Despite this abysmal success rate, many people – either out of desperation or misplaced hope – still take such programmes seriously and spend large amounts of time, emotion and, crucially, money on diets ranging from the almost sensible to the entirely nonsensical. There are currently more than ten thousand diet books for sale on Amazon.com, and the diet industry in the US alone is worth in excess of €50 billion annually. Figures for Ireland are harder to come by but estimates suggest it can be measured in tens of millions of euro, and even the most casual look at bookshop shelves groaning under the weight of diet books suggests that our appetite for the quick-fix diet is equally insatiable.

There are books, courses, television programmes, websites and, increasingly, surgical procedures all aimed at helping people to slim. Critics believe that the diet industry is more about exploitation than helping people lose weight. One dietician I spoke to reviewed twelve diet books for a television programme and found all of them to be useless. When celebrities with personal trainers, lifestyle gurus and nutritionists on twenty-four-hour standby constantly move from faddy diet to faddy diet and still struggle to shed the pounds, and then keep them off, what chance do the rest of us have? None at all.

There was a widely reported story in the British press recently about a thirty-one-year-old woman who estimated that she had wasted an astonishing £200,000 on diets over the last twenty years but that, despite this 'investment', had yo-yoed between 12 stone and 19 stone – without ever reaching the size 12 dress size that she craves.

While the sums she has spent are on the high side (to put it very mildly!), the woman is not that unusual. People inclined towards obsessive dieting can expect to spend tens of thousands of euro over the course of their lifetime on trying – and usually failing – to get in shape, according to a recent survey by women's magazine More. Experts estimate that, on average, it costs around £150 to lose just one pound of fat. It costs a whole lot less, however, to put it back on.

Savings: Incalculable

Up in smoke

Unquestionably, the stupidest thing I have ever done was to start smoking – which I then continued to do for close to two decades. I've calculated that, over the eighteen years that I smoked, I probably spent €45,854, give or take a few euro – just typing that sum makes me very sad – and got absolutely nothing in return except more colds, worse coughs, higher stress levels, bad breath, and a lifelong fear that the physical damage the smoking did to my lungs will come back to haunt me sooner or later.

I completely stopped smoking nearly three years ago, and in that time have saved myself €7,500. If you smoke, stop. You will then have done more to improve you finances than by following all the other tips in this book – and several other books like it – combined.

If you are in the process of giving up the fags and are using nicotine-replacement therapies, you will have noticed how ridiculously expensive nicotine gum, inhalers and patches are. It will come as no surprise that we are being completely ripped off when it comes these products, which cost almost 50 percent less in the North than they do on the southern side of the border.

There is a way you can reduce the cost. Let's say a packet of seven 10 milligram nicotine patches cost €20. How much do you think a packet of seven 5 milligram patches will cost? That's right, €20. So if you're using the 5 milligram patches to give up cigarettes – and it worked for me – then why not buy the 10 milligram patches, cut them in half, and cut the bill by half.

Total savings this month: €180

Healthy options

The Health Insurance Authority has carried out extensive research which reveals that Irish consumers find it very difficult to understand health-insurance products. The complexity of the different policies on offer, with the different levels of cover and their different excesses, might explain why so many people with health insurance – 1.6 million people, in fact – stick with the VHI, despite the fact that it is the most expensive health insurer on the market.

Of course, the VHI will point out that it is a not-for-profit organization, talk up its payout policy and bleat on about the risk-equalisation problems of recent years, and that's fair enough, but all consumers really should care about, as long as the policies of the rival companies are broadly similar and right for them, is the bottom line. Families can save nearly €300 a year by moving their family health-insurance plan from one company to another. The cost of covering a family on VHI's Plan B – its best-selling scheme – is €1,813.16 a year, while a family on Vivas's We Plan Level 2 will currently pay €1,541, or €272 less a year.

Shortly after Christmas, I received a letter from Quinn Healthcare telling me that my health-insurance policy was due for renewal. In honeyed tones, it thanked me for my business and assured me in big bold letters that there was *'No need to do a thing'*. 'We would like to inform you of a number of changes that may affect your policy,' it went on to say. The first thing was that the cost of the policy was increasing – the letter did not bother telling me by how much – either in percentage or actual terms. Then I was told that 'in line with government recommendations', Quinn Healthcare was introducing 'a standard, transparent and uniform price through the removal of discount schemes'. Hmm, that sounds a bit worrying, I thought. The letter went on to say that if I paid by installments, 'a 3 percent credit charge will now apply'.

'We are committed to keeping prices competitive and compared to other insurers in the market we have kept this increase as low as possible', the letter concluded. As low as possible! They increased my premiums by 18 percent when their 5 percent price hike, the abolition of the 10 percent discount I got for being a member of a credit union (something they blame the goverment for), and the 3

percent credit charge for paying by direct debit were factored in. (Isn't it peculiar how NTL decided to penalise people for not paying by direct debit, while Quinn now penalises them for paying using the system?)

So I took myself off to Vivas, which quoted me a price of €678 compared to €848 with Quinn – a saving of €170 a year by making a single phone call and sending off one cancellation letter.

The main consideration for most people when it comes to health insurance centres on the level of hospital care and accommodation that is covered. What they usually want to know is whether they will get private or semi-private care, and whether they will get access to the more salubrious private hospitals, such as the Blackrock Clinic and the Mater Private. (Of course, when people think 'semi-private', they probably envisage a room with two beds, whereas in reality semi-private means a room with six beds, which makes it pretty public, but that is neither here nor there.) The other thing to consider is the level of outpatient care and maternity care a policy offers.

Let's look at the entry-level product offered by all three insurers. This gives you semi-private care in our public hospitals. Quinn's Essential costs €31.78 per month. The VHI's Plan A is €38.59, while Vivas's Me Level 1 is €27.66. So the difference in price between the cheapest and the dearest is €10.93 a month, which, spread out over a year, comes to €131.16.

Probably the most common policy is the mid-level one, which covers you for private rooms if they are available in the public hospitals, and semi-private rooms in the private hospitals. VHI's Plan B costs €55.39, Essential Plus from Quinn is €51.58, and Vivas's I and We Level 2 is €46.33. So, €9.06 a month difference

between the cheapest and the dearest, which is €108.72 per year.

Then you have the Rolls Royce packages – the ones that cover all the private hospitals. The Quinn Healthcare Health Manager Gold will cost you a fairly hefty €166.09 a month. Vivas's I and We Level 5 is €153.50, while Plan E from the VHI costs €169.63. That's a difference of €16.03 a month, or €193.56 a year. Although in truth, if you can afford the very top policies, you probably won't be too concerned about the two hundred quid.

In all three categories, the VHI comes out bottom of the pile. Now, these prices do come with a health warning, if you'll forgive the choice of words. Then there are excesses that should be borne in mind, and some companies offer sweeteners like a degree of dental cover – the VHI have such an add-on – or cheap travel insurance, so you need to be sure that the policy you're paying for is right for you and your family.

Legislation protects your right to switch health-insurance providers without penalty, and you can switch health insurer without serving waiting periods if your gap in cover is less than thirteen weeks, you're not going for an upgrade of cover, and you have served all your waiting period with your old insurer.

If your insurer leaves the market for any reason, it is obliged to continue covering you until your next renewal date, and you will be able to switch to another insurer at any time without penalty, providing the above conditions are met. If you switch health insurers to a policy with a similar level of cover while being treated for an illness, your cover will not be affected.

The Health Insurance Authority has a website which provides pretty clear and impartial price guidelines, allowing consumers to make like-for-like comparisons on the various packages the companies offer.

Saving: At least €120

Table 1: Hospital Accommodation – Quinn Healthcare, VHI Healthcare, and VIVAS Health

Cost per month incl. Vhi and Vivas Adult Group Rate discount (net of tax relief at source)	Product	Public Hospitals		Private Hospitals (excl. Hi-Tech Hospitals)		Hi-tech Hospitals*	
		Semi-private Room	Private Room	Semi-private Room	Private Room	Semi-private Room	Private Room
QUINN HEALTHCARE							
€31.75	Essential	✓					
€46.26	Essential Plus with Excess	✓	✓	€80 excess			
€51.58	Essential Plus	✓	✓	✓			
€51.41/€56.22	PersonalCare/Familycare	✓	✓	€150 excess			
€47.03	HealthManager Starter	✓	✓	A limited number of private hospitals are covered			
€70.72	HealthManager	✓	✓	€126 excess	€126 excess		
€166.09	HealthManager Gold	✓	✓	✓	✓	✓	✓
VHI HEALTHCARE							
€38.59 / 40.53	Plan A / Plan A Option	✓					
€44.82/ €45.70	First Plan** / Family Plan **	✓	✓				
€55.39/60.06	Plan B / Plan B Option	✓	✓	✓			
€55.64/56.54	First Plan Plus** / Family Plan Plus**	✓	✓	✓***			
€86.95/90.16	Plan C / Plan C Option	✓	✓	✓	✓		
€90.22	Forward Plan **	✓	✓	✓	✓		
€115.27	Plan D	✓	✓	✓	✓	✓	
€169.63	Plan E	✓	✓	✓	✓	✓	✓
€10.42	HealthSteps Silver	These products do not provide cover for hospital accommodation and can be bought alone or in conjunction with another policy.					
€15.87	HealthSteps Gold						
VIVAS HEALTH							
€27.66	Me Level 1	✓					
€32.50	I & We Level 1	✓					
€43.13	Me level 2	✓	✓	✓			
€46.33	I & We Level 2	✓	✓	✓			
€71.04	I & We Level 3	✓	✓	✓	✓		
€110.33	I & We Level 4	✓	✓	✓	✓	✓	
€153.50	I & We Level 5	✓	✓	✓	✓	✓	✓
€10.75	Day-to-day Me	These products do not provide cover for hospital accommodation. Me Day-to-Day can be purchased with a hospital plan at a saving of €1.84 per month. Level A/We Day-to-day products can be purchased with a hospital plan at a saving of €1.75 per month. Day to Day 50 can be purchased with a hospital plan at a saving of €2.75 per month						
€11.91	Day-to-day I & We Level A						
€18.54	Day-to-day 50						

Prices Correct as of the 10th January 2008

Cheaper and nicer

Add up the price of all those lunchtime sandwiches eaten at your desk over the course of a year, and the cost will climb alarmingly. Let's say you spend €5 a day on your sarnie (hardly excessive in modern Ireland); after a year – not counting time off for holidays, bank holidays and one week's sick leave – you will have spent €1,100.

Meanwhile, a year's supply of bread, ham and cheese to make your own sandwiches would have set you back just €300. The vegetables needed to make home-made soup, which can be frozen and brought into work on occasion, will cost even less.

And while I'm not Jamie Oliver or anything, here are a couple of soup recipes that even the most kitchen-phobic person could probably manage.

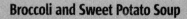

Broccoli and Sweet Potato Soup

A couple of broccoli heads (chopped) (€3)
Four sweet potatoes (peeled and chopped) (€2)
An onion (chopped) €0.50
Two litres of chicken stock (€0.60)
A couple of glugs of olive oil (€0.10)
Salt and pepper (free, well almost)

Fry the onions. Then add the broccoli and the sweet potatoes. Fry them for a bit and add the stock. Allow it all to boil away merrily for around twenty minutes. Then whoosh it in the pot with a hand blender, and there you have in – six wholesome portions of soup for your lunch for just over €6, and twenty-five minutes of your time.

Leek and Potato Soup

Four leeks (chopped) (€4)
Three potatoes (chopped) (€1)
An onion (chopped) (€0.50)
Couple of glugs of olive oil (€0.10)
Salt and pepper

Fry the onions, and when they're soft add the chopped potatoes and the sliced leeks. Fry them for a bit and add the stock. Allow it all to boil away merrily for around twenty minutes, then whoosh it in the pot with a hand blender, and you have another six portions of soup for your lunch for just over a fiver, and twenty-five minutes of your time.

Apart from the price considerations, there is also the question of taste and health. Pre-packaged sandwiches which have been left sweating in their plastic coffins for days on the shelves of your local supermarket might be convenient but they are not, by any stretch of the imagination, pleasant to eat.

Now I am nothing if not realistic, and the chances of any of us, with the exception, perhaps, of the Penny Pinchers, getting it together to make lunchtime sandwiches or soup five days a week every week for the rest of the year is slim. So let's set the bar a little lower. Three days a week you can splash out on store-filled bagels, salads or whatever else takes your fancy, and make your own lunch just twice a week. The savings will still be substantial.

Savings: €300

Coffee docked

Coffee is another ridiculously priced item we are increasingly happy to waste our money on every day. While the prices vary from coffee shop to coffee shop, a large coffee is likely to set you back at least €2.50 – and in case you've ever wondered, the cost to the coffee seller is rarely over 40 cent, and their mark-up can be as much as 1,000 percent. Have one of them every morning as you arrive bleary-eyed into work, and you'll spend €700 over the next twelve months. A coffee plunger, on the other hand, will cost you €30, a year's supply of freshly ground coffee will cost another €150, and the hot water will be virtually free, taking your total savings on coffee over a single year to €520. Again, there's no point in insisting that you never drink coffee-shop-bought coffee again, so the savings will in fact be slightly less.

Incidentally, the sums we casually throw away on takeaway coffee has given the world a new phrase: 'the latte factor'. It's an American idea which is based on the notion that if you pay closer attention to the small things you buy daily and cut out some, such as the pricey lattes, bottled water, glossy magazines and the like, you can save your self a fortune without any great hardship.

Let's say you spend a fiver a day, five days a week, on a latte and a muffin: you will spend €25 a week, which works out at €52,000 over the course of your working life. If, instead, you deposited that €100 every month in an account promising a return of just 5 percent, at the end of the same forty years your daily coffee and muffin would have turned into several hundred thousand euro.

Savings: €260

Write it down

There must be a good reason that the very first tip in virtually every money-saving guide stresses the need to write down exactly what you're spending your money on, in order better to gauge where the waste is. It's not the easiest thing to do – the pen and paper are never close at hand when you're blowing the average monthly wage of a Caribbean islander on a late-night Mojito – but it is still worth trying to keep a log. If you can't write everything down immediately, just get into the habit of asking for receipts for all your purchases, and at the end of each day, add them up. By the end of a month, you'll be able to see exactly where all your money is going.

Total savings this month: €680

Month 3

Shopped

The major supermarkets in Ireland all claim to offer consumers the most amazing bargains, but a National Consumer Agency survey published last summer revealed the lie in their advertising. It showed that there's almost no difference in the prices charged by the three main multiples, Tesco, Dunnes Stores and Superquinn.

For a basket of forty-five branded items, the difference between the cheapest and the dearest was only €2.20, or 1.6 percent. The kindest explanation for this is that they're all watching each other very closely in the race to provide us with ever better bargains. The reality may be that the major supermarkets are operating an informal cartel – or, more likely, that the absence of real competition means they don't have to bother lowering their prices.

It's different across the border, where retailers such as ASDA, now owned by the US giant Walmart, seems genuinely to drive down prices. Supermarket prices in Newry are, at the very least, 15 percent cheaper than in the same supermarkets a few kilometres away in Dundalk. The retailers bleat on about higher overheads and higher rates of VAT in the Republic but then refuse to let the public have even the merest glimpse of their annual accounts, so that we have to take it as a matter of trust. And they've done a whole lot to earn our trust over the last thirty years, now, haven't they?

Despite the meanness of the supermarkets, there are ways to save yourself money on your shopping. First up, forget the loyalty (but not the loyalty cards – sign up to the lot of them, they'll save you around €100 a year). Being loyal to Tesco, Dunnes, Superquinn, or even Marks & Spencer – bless them and their lovely food and less lovely prices – is just stupid, plain and simple. When it comes to saving money, there is nothing more important than shopping round.

And pay special attention to the German retailers Lidl and Aldi. Love them or loathe them, both are very cheap, and while not everything they sell is nice – or even barely tolerable – they still offer great savings on certain items. Cleaning products, for instance. Is there anyone who is loyal to a particular brand of bleach? I mean, really? A one-litre tub of Domestos costs €3.17 in Lidl, while a similarly sized tub of bleach in Aldi costs €1.29 . It's the same for bin bags, sponges, rubber gloves and a whole lot of other items. If you buy just twenty items in either Aldi or Lidl each week, instead of buying branded products, you'll shave 30 percent off your weekly shopping bill for those items.

If, for instance, you have a cat that likes Whiskas, then you can expect to spend €350 this year on its food. Quietly swap it for Aldi's Vitacat Supreme Chunks, and you'll spend only €115. Your cat won't notice.

And it's not just the cat who should be expected to economise. If you routinely buy sparkling water and swap the four-pack of 1.5-litre bottles of Ballygowan – price €5.16 – for the Comeragh Springs four-pack from Aldi – price €1.99 – then over the course of a year you could save yourself another €150.

Incidentally, it's important to remember that there are occasions when quality does count. Cheap brands don't always offer better value. For more than three years now, I

Aldi Vs Brand Names

Kitchen cleaner	Power Force Kitchen Cleaner (€1.19 / 750ml)
Bleach	Power Force Thick Bleach (€1.29 / 2 litres)
Bin bags	Alio Tie Handle Refuse Sacks (€1.99 / 20 pack)
Rubber gloves	Rubber Gloves (€1.49 / 3 pack)
Cleaning sponges	Power Force Fingertip Scourers (€0.89 / 8 pack)
Tin foil	Alio Kitchen Foil (€2.29 / 30 metres)
Clingfilm	Alio Extra Wide Clingfilm (€1.79 / 75 metres)
Cleaning cloths	Power Force Dishcloths (€1.79 / 6 pack)
Household sponges	Power Force Antibacterial Cleaner (€0.99 / 500ml)
Cleaner spray	Power Force Glass Cleaner (€0.99 / 500ml)
Total	**€14.70**

Meanwhile in our local Tesco:

Kitchen cleaner	Muscle Kitchen Cleaner Multi Task (€2.99 / 750ml)
Bleach	Domestos (€3.17 / 2 litres)
Bin bags	Tesco Drawstring Large Refuse Sacks (€2.59 / 20 pack)
Rubber gloves	Marigold Futura Rubber Gloves (€4.41 / 8 pack)
Cleaning sponges	Boyne Valley Non Stick Scourers (€0.95 / 3 pack)
Tin foil	Raytex Kitchen Foil (€7.13 / 445mm x 30m)
Clingfilm	Raytex Clingfilm (€4.80 / 100m)
Cleaning cloths	Tesco Dish Cloth (€2.45 / 4 pack)
Household sponges	Dettol Antibac Surface Cleaner Spray (€2.79 / 500ml)
Cleaner spray	Mr Muscle Window Cleaner Spray (€1.77 / 500ml)
Total	**€33.05**

have been reviewing products as part of 'Pricewatch' in the Irish Times, and in only one in five product tests does the cheapest brand come out on top. Take washing-up liquid. There is no one who could seriously argue that the Lidl or Aldi brand is as good as Fairy liquid. That august consumer body Which? has consistently ranked Fairy as the best product on the market, despite its higher cost. A single one-litre bottle cleans more dirty plates – 11,000 – than any of its rivals.

Five shopping habits to break . . .

- *Chicken pieces with the skin on* are about half the price of pre-skinned chicken pieces. Removing the skin takes seconds, and you'll have saved yourself a euro handily enough.

- *Bagged salad* Yes, yes, yes, it's handy, but bagged salads costs ten times the price of making the salad up from scratch, and it doesn't taste half as nice. And one of the reasons it doesn't taste so good is because it has been washed in all manner of chemicals which not only take all the dirt away but clean the leaves of most of their nutrients too. Nice. Oh, and if you do buy salad leaves, either bagged or otherwise, please remember to eat them. According to a survey carried out by a British insurance company a couple of years ago, 61 percent of people polled confessed to binning a soggy lettuce every week because they bought it under the false assumption that they'd eat more greens than they actually did.

- *Pre-grated cheese* What's that about? A kilogramme of grated Cheddar costs €14.45, while a block of the same cheese from the same company costs around €4 less. Presuming that you are already in possession of a cheese grater, you've saved yourself €2 on a single block of the stuff.

- *Ready meals* You're in Marks and Spencer and there's a ready-to-cook meal sitting there, demanding to be put into your trolley. Just say no. Ready-made meals can be more than five times as expensive as the constituent parts of that meal in the same supermarket which are on the shelves just a few metres away. And it really doesn't take that much effort to fry a steak and bake a potato, even if the Cook/GastroPub/Finest range has been tarted up to look super-tasty.

• And make sure you never go shopping when you're hungry – you'll end up buying a whole lot more than you intended if you do.

. . . and four to develop

• *Learn the prices of the basics* How much is a litre of milk? If you can't answer immediately, how are you supposed to know you're being ripped off when you're local corner shop charges you €2.50 for it.

• *Always bring a loyalty card with you* And you can be loyal to as many different supermarkets as you like – except for the Aldis and Lidls of the world, who don't care for such frippery.

• *Special offers save you money* Always take advantage of the buy-one-get-one-free offers (as long as what you're buying isn't perishable). As an experiment some time this month, and for one shop only, try to buy only items which are on special offer. You'll be amazed by the savings that you can make.

• *Make a list* Our major supermarkets pay people buckets of money to work out the best ways to get us to part with our cash, and while we may think we're immune to the soothing background music, the judiciously placed 'offers' and the smell of baking which wafts through the aisles, the bill at the checkout would beg to differ. That's why it's important to make lists and stick rigidly to them. Not only will it be cheaper, it'll make the trip to the supermarket a lot shorter too.

Pop quiz

How much does a litre of milk cost? Or a pound of butter, a sliced pan, a block of cheese or a box of Barry's tea bags? There was a time when everyone knew the price of all the staples, which meant that it was more difficult for retailers to rip people off. It you knew that a pint of milk normally costs €0.30, and suddenly you were being asked for €0.50, you'd be a lot more likely to just walk away. Now we haven't a clue how much any of this stuff costs, so when a smiling chap in your local convenience store asks you for €15 and your first-born child for a couple of litres of milk and some cheese, you just hand it over without a moment's hesitation.

How much do you think these ten items cost in your local Tesco?

1. Kerrygold butter 454g
2. Premier milk 1 litre
3. Kilmeaden Red Cheddar 400g
4. Barrys Classic tea bags 80pk 250g
5. Nescafé Gold Blend coffee 100g
6. Diet Coke 330ml
7. McVities Rich Tea 200g
8. 1 kg Rooster potatoes
9. 1 Golden Delicious apple
10. 1 kg round steak minced

Answers on page 40

A spring in your step

If possible, you should leave the car at home and walk or cycle to work. This is not to say that you should abandon the warmth and dryness of your car or the train or bus on a winter's morning when it's lashing down outside, but on days when the forecast isn't bad you should consider changing the way you commute. Some time back, for an article for the Irish Times Motoring supplement, I, on foot, raced the Motoring editor and his very fancy car to work from the leafy suburb of Ranelagh – a place, incidentally, where neither of us can actually afford to live. I beat him by nearly twenty minutes, and that was at a gentle stroll rather that at a sprint, just in case you think I arrived in the office drenched in sweat and gasping for breath. Not only will putting your best foot forward save you money, it'll keep you fitter and save you money on the gym. There is a limit to how far you can walk, however, and if you live in Lucan and work near O'Connell Street, you might want to consider buying a bike instead.

Pop Quiz Answers

1. €2.25	**2.** €0.99	**3.** €5.09
4. €3.15	**5.** €3.91	**6.** €0.66
7. €1.24	**8.** €1.59	**9.** €0.47
10. €9.29		

Eating out without splashing out

There are absolutely loads of really great restaurants in Ireland offering incredible food at rock-bottom prices.

No, only joking, of course there aren't. While there are certainly a small number of really good-value, high-quality restaurants to be found, the vast majority of them – at least the vast majority of the ones I have eaten in – offer fairly ordinary fare at fairly extraordinary prices. The food always costs too much, the wine lists rarely have anything for less than €20 – even though many of the bottles are instantly recognisable as being available in most bog standard off-licences for less than half that price – and the mineral water has increased by at least a factor of six on the short journey from the wholesalers to your table.

When it comes to eating out, it is hard to figure out ways to save money without skipping the starter and the dessert or doing a runner when the waiter's back is turned – and I wouldn't recommend you doing either of those things. But there are little ways in which you can reduce your bill.

The first thing to do is not buy the bottled water. There are many ordinary restaurants in Dublin that think they can get away with charging more than €6 for a 700ml bottle of water. The reason they do get away with it most of the time is because we let them. Maybe it's because we're intimidated by the fact that we're in strange surroundings, or maybe because we don't want to seem cheap, but too often when the waiter sidles up to the table as we are just opening the menu to offer a 'choice' of sparking or still water while we decide which overpriced items to eat tonight, we don't ask for tap water. Who cares if they look at you disapprovingly: the public water system here is fine (readers from Galway look away now), so why not take advantage of it. You can always judge a good-value restaurant that is actually thinking about its diners' best interests if, in addition to offering you sparkling and still water, they give you a third choice of tap.

Early-bird and pre-theatre menus can prove to be very affordable, so if it doesn't really matter what time you eat, this is the way to go. The early-bird option is not always the best one, however: if you're bringing someone on a romantic night out, booking the table for 6.30 pm and having only two courses may not be the best way to make a good impression.

I asked a restaurant owner for some tips on eating out on the cheap, and he was stumped. Eventually he came up with this idea. Keep an eye out for new restaurants in your area which are just about to open to the public. Before they do, make contact and express an interest in their menus. Chances are, he tells me, that at the very least you'll be offered some vouchers to eat in the opening week, and you may even get a free meal out of it. While there's nothing wrong with this idea, I was a bit depressed that this was the best he could come up with: it's a bit too Mr Thrifty for my liking.

He also suggested that it was worth complaining if things were not exactly as you wanted them to be. In a good restaurant, if your complaint is legitimate, they'll knock something off your bill. I would not recommend this as a long-term strategy, however. I'm not sure how seriously your complaints would be taken if you found something new to moan about in your favourite restaurant every single Friday night.

If you want to eat in the best of Irish restaurants but don't want to have to re-mortgage your house to do so, forget about the evening menus and just go for lunch. Here's an example: many people would consider Restaurant Patrick Guilbaud, with its two Michelin stars, to be the finest restaurant in the country. And, in my humble opinion, they wouldn't be far wrong. It is a great restaurant. And also, sadly, a very expensive one. Except when you take advantage of their lunchtime deals. You'll pay not much more than €30 for two courses – two courses which will taste as good as the evening meals which cost at least twice that price.

Total savings this month: €50

Month 4

Would you credit it?

The most important money-saving tip I can think of when it comes to your credit card is don't use it, or if you do use it, make sure you clear the balance every month. Credit cards are one of the banking sector's greatest cash cows, and most institutions who issue them make huge profits thanks to our lack of self-control and sheer laziness. I came across a tip once which suggested that I keep my credit card at the bottom of an ice-cube tray which is then frozen solid, to make impulse purchases impossible. (Before buying anything, I would have to wait for the ice to melt.) This seems a bit extreme, but there is a certain degree of sense in not having your credit card immediately to hand.

Make sure you're getting the best deal on your credit card, and if you're not, switch: while loyalty is certainly a commendable trait, being loyal to a credit-card company is perhaps one of the stupidest things we can do – yet most of us, because of inertia, do it as a matter of routine. Don't let them get away with it.

Always pay attention to the APR, or Annual Percentage Rate. The APR is the standard measure for the cost of loans. Briefly – and for the sake of the man in the Financial Regulator's ad, who confessed in shamed tones to not knowing what an APR was – it's the gross amount of compound interest charged if you don't make any repayments on a loan. So if you make one single purchase of €100 on your credit card in a year and don't pay anything for twelve months, you'll still owe the original €100 plus another amount, say €20, in interest, giving an APR of 20 percent. The APR on purchases and ATM withdrawals can vary by as much as 100 percent depending on which card you chose, so making the wrong choice could cost you a packet. According to recent figures, the APR on purchases ranges from 9.1 percent to 19.1 percent, while the interest applied on ATM withdrawals made with your credit card (never a bright thing to do, but sometimes you have no option) range from 9.4 percent to 20.7 percent. If you do switch to a new credit-card provider, make sure to transfer or pay off any balance on your previous card and, critically, close your previous credit-card account.

Not only does it pay to shop around, it might also be worth borrowing to clear the balance. According to figures from the Financial Regulator, the total cost of a €3,500 loan repaid over twelve months can be as little as €133 – significantly less than the cost of maintaining a credit-card loan. Of course, the most important thing to remember about borrowing to clear your credit-card debt is to not let the credit card bill mount up again almost immediately, leaving you with two loans instead of one.

The Financial Regulator carries frequently updated surveys of credit cards on its website, itsyourmoney.ie, and is always worth a visit.

Credit card

This survey contains up-to-date information from individual firms. See our personal loans and credit section for more credit information. Please read our disclaimer before you use our information.

Financial institution	Product (click on the links for further information)	APR % charged on purchases	APR % charged on cash withdrawals	Cash advance fee: minimum % of transaction	Over credit card limit fee
AIB	'be' Credit Card	15.15% or 18.15%[1]	19.92%	1.5% (Min €1.90)[2]	€2.54
	Platinum	11.5%	13.17%	1.5% (Min €1.90)[3]	€2.54
American Express	American Express Blue[4]	19.1%	20.2%	1.5% (Min €2.54)[5]	€10.16[6]
Bank of Ireland	Platinum Advantage	14.9%[7]	16.5%[7]	1.5% (Min €2.54)[5]	Nil
	2 in 1	15.9%	17.4%	1.5% (Min €2.54)[5]	€7.50[6]
EBS	Member[8]	10.9%	16.7%	1.5% (Min €1.90, Max €31.74)[2]	€12.70
First Active	First Active MasterCard	12.9%	20.1%	1.5% (Min €2.54)[2]	€8.50
GE Money	Debenhams MasterCard	17.90%	19.90%	1.5% (Min €2.50)[2]	€12.70
Halifax	Halifax Credit Card	9.5%	11.2%	1.5% (Min €1.90)	€7.00
MBNA	Standard	16.9%	19.9%	1.5% (Min €1.90, max €31.74)[2]	€12.70
	Platinum	13.9%	19.9%	1.5% (Min €1.90, Max €31.74)[2]	€12.70
National Irish Bank	Standard Card[9]	10.2%	10.2%	1.5% (Min €2.00)	NIL
	Gold[10]	9.4%	9.4%	1.5% (Min €2.00)	NIL
One Direct	Standard[11]	16.9%	19.9%	1.5% (Min €1.90, Max €31.74)[2]	€12.70
	Platinum[11]	13.9%	19.9%	1.5% (Min €1.90, Max €31.74)[2]	€12.70
Permanent TSB	ICE	9.9%	11.6%	1.5% (Min €2.00)	NIL
Tesco Personal Finance	Classic	14.9%	16.7%	1.5% (Min €1.90)[2]	€6.35
Ulster Bank	Standard	16.5%	20.7%	1.5% (Min €2.54)[2]	€8.50
	Zinc	13.4%	17.5%	1.5% (Min €2.54)[2]	€8.50

1. Lower rate of 15.15% APR applies to cardholders with purchases equal to or exceeding €5,000 and higher rate of 18.15% APR applies to cardholders with purchases not exceeding €5,000 in a 12 month assessment period. Incur two or more penalty fees within a 12 month assessment period and interest will be charged at the higher APR from the next statement regardless of spend. Higher rate of 18.15% APR also applies to existing AIB customers for first 12 months.
2. This charge is also applied when account is in credit.
3. Applies if withdrawal results in a debit balance.
4. Issued by Bank of Ireland under licence.
5. No cash advance fee applies if account is in credit or has zero balance after cash withdrawal is processed.
6. A charge applies in relation to any statement period in which one or more overlimit positions have occurred.
7. Based on a credit limit of €6,350 and inclusive of an annual fee of €76.18 payable on Platinum Advantage.
8. To avail of this credit card you must be a member of the EBS. This card is issued by MBNA.
9. In conjunction with Freedom Customer Package.
10. In conjunction with NIB Easy Plus Customer Package, a quarterly fee of €18.75 is charged.
11. Card issued by MBNA.

Please note: In addition to the non-euro purchases/withdrawals fee, some institutions may apply a further fee where an agency is used for currency conversion. Use our Jargon Buster, if you need an explanation of financial terms in plain English.

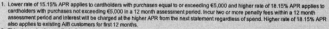

Do you really need it?

Impulse shopping is the enemy of the budget-conscious – not to mention a sure way of accumulating vast quantities of junk in your house. Don't allow yourself to fall victim to this pernicious habit. Never buy clothes on the spur of the moment; instead, give yourself a twenty-four-hour cooling-off period (even if you can't be bothered with the ice tray), and if after that time you still find yourself thinking about those boots or that mulcher, then go and buy it by all means.

Ink about it

While the ink cartridges used for photograph-quality ink-jet printers for home use can't actually print money, people who use them often wish they did, as they cost so much and need to be replaced so often. Anyone who has bought themselves a printer

for €60 only to realise that the replacement cartridges needed to keep them printing cost at least as much again will not be surprised to learn that, by volume, the ink is almost seven times more expensive than some vintage champagnes.

In fact, printer ink is so expensive that a recent investigation in the US uncovered a healthy trade in fake branded cartridges, putting it right up there with Gucci handbags and Rolex watches as the counterfeit item of choice for many criminals.

When digital cameras became affordable and the quality of colour printers improved dramatically, consumers started looking forward to unlimited cheap photographs printed instantly at home. But it was not to be. A single high-quality A4 colour photograph can use more than €1 worth of ink, depending on the printer, while an A4 sheet of photo-quality paper will cost around €0.50.

One of the reasons cartridges are so expensive is that many printer manufacturers sell the hardware at a loss and rely on the cartridges to ensure long-term profits. In fact, some companies can make as much as 90 percent of their profits from the sale of ink cartridges. They are so loath to see people circumventing the need to buy high-cost replacements that many will void warranties if generic inks or refills are used, and some have actually started installing chips in an attempt to force users to rely on their branded cartridges. Some manufacturers have even gone so far as to develop 'cartridge-killing' technology which will fuse a cartridge and render it useless once the amount of ink falls below a certain level. This is objectionable not just from the perspective of financially strapped consumers: there are serious environmental concerns

about developing products with such an extreme level of built-in obsolescence.

There are ways to make savings. Unless high-quality prints are essential, the draft printing mode should always be selected, and if colour is not completely necessary, documents should be printed in greyscale. Generic ink cartridges are significantly cheaper than brand names, while having cartridges refilled rather than replaced can cost as much as 60 percent less.

When buying a printer, a good rule of thumb is: the cheaper the printer the dearer the cartridge. Make sure to ask what the price per page of using each printer is. If they don't know, don't buy it. Some companies display the information on their websites, while reviews of other models can be easily found online and will have the information there as a matter of course. Work out roughly how many pages you will want to print per week, and then work out the cost over a couple of years.

Above all else, when buying a printer, make sure to get the one that meets your needs, and not one the store wants to sell you. If you don't want to print in colour, a good black-and-white laser printer costs around €100. They are faster, cost less to run, and produce clearer text than ink-jet printers. Entry-level colour laser printers cost from €200, and while they cannot print photos they are fine for simple graphics.

You a can also save money (and do a small bit for the environment) by printing less, reusing printer paper and printing on both sides of a page. And remember, if you are printing a document of, say, fifty pages and your computer tells you that there is not enough ink, all it means is that there may not be enough ink for fifty pages. If you print the document in batches of five pages, chances are that there will be enough.

Nine modern practices to make you despair

From handling charges to baggage charges and confusing price tags to inflated drug costs, big business is increasingly savvy at extracting money from Irish consumers. Here are nine ways they do it, in no particular order.

Tag trickery

You're in Gap and happen across a shirt you like. It's not expensive, so you join the queue and wait patiently for your turn at the till. When it comes, the cashier scans the item and does some natty folding before asking for a whole lot more money than you expected. There's been a mistake, you think – and you're right. The problem is, it's yours: you've been looking at the sterling price on the tag. Gap, Dunnes, Top Shop and dozens of other multiples may not be intentionally trying to mislead their customers by displaying (lower) sterling prices so prominently, but it certainly feels like that sometimes. And although many people think otherwise, if you see a price on the shelf that is lower than the price at the till (because the label only carries the Sterling price), you don't have the right to get it for the cheaper price in euro.

'Handling' fees

While no one disputes the right of companies such as Ticketmaster to make a profit, do they really have to make quite so much off the back of each of their customers? The long-standing practice of imposing handling charges on each ticket rather than each transaction is ridiculous, and becoming more and more widespread, as theatres, sports clubs and cinemas join the booking-fee bonanza. Recently, Ticketmaster introduced a Ticketfast booking

system, which sees it sending out e-mails in lieu of actual tickets. With no postage, printing or handling costs of any kind associated with the service, Ticketmaster is making substantial savings, which they've passed on to consumers. Only joking, of course – they haven't.

Credit-card chicanery

Credit-card surcharges have rightly been called anti-consumer, discriminatory and mean-spirited by the Consumer Association of Ireland and anyone else who has shelled out between 1 and 5 percent extra when buying a ticket or booking a holiday with their credit card. The retailers involved claim that they're just passing on the fees levied by the credit-card companies – an assertion that is disputed by consumer lobbyists. The Minister for Enterprise and Employment, Micheál Martin, is set to ban surcharges by the end of 2008 – by which time the service providers affected will presumably have worked out an entirely different way to make us pay that little bit more.

The percentage game

The property market may be in decline, but estate agents' fees are not. Ten years ago, if you sold a house in a leafy Dublin suburb for IR£100,000, you could expect to pay IR£2,000 to your estate agent. Today (but perhaps not tomorrow), the house is selling for a million euro, which means that the estate agent is now making twenty grand for doing exactly the same amount of work as before. Consumers could be forgiven for asking why the estate agents can't charge flat fees. (Exactly the same thing applies to solicitors, by the way, but they have deep pockets, keen minds, are terribly precious, and have a much greater understanding of the libel laws than estate agents, so it's best not to say anything bad about them. Except, perhaps, to point out that when it comes to most property deals, our solicitors are thieving scoundrels. According to a report published earlier this year by the Consumers Association of Ireland, conveyancing fees in Ireland are double what they are in the UK, and while fees have fallen in recent years, Irish solicitors still rank amongst the most expensive in the EU. In some respects, it is not entirely their fault: solicitors are the only profession which is legally allowed to carry out conveyancing, despite the fact that when it comes to some properties, a four-year-old armed with little more than a few colouring pencils and an Iggle Piggle doll could probably manage it. The Competition Authority has called for the sector to be opened up, so we'll wait and see what happens on this score.

No-fair airlines

While Ryanair is to be commended for doing more than any other company to bring down the price of air travel, it is to be condemned for taking the joy out of travelling. I probably get more complaints about Ryanair (well, it's a toss-up between them and NTL, if truth be told), with people routinely complaining about obnoxious staff, ridiculous add-ons, and the introduction of 'weight police' who live to catch people travelling with a few kilos more than the meagre Ryanair baggage allowance permits.

Flights with a price tag of a single euro can end up costing over sixty times that when taxes, airport charges, credit-card surcharges, wheelchair surcharges and baggage-handling surcharges are factored in. Not to be left behind, Aer Lingus has been slavishly following Ryanair's charging policies and adding a few more of

their own, including the ridiculous premium for certain seats on their planes.

In 2007, Ryanair increased its baggage and airport check-in charges and issued a warning that it will continue to increase them in an effort to 'encourage' its passengers to travel with hand luggage only. Baggage charges have gone up from €6 to €9 per bag, while check-in fees have increased from €3 to €4. A spokesman said the move was to encourage passengers to avoid the charges by bringing hand luggage only and checking in online, which is free. He said the airline would keep increasing its charges until it had reached its target of having at least half of its passengers travelling with hand luggage only.

Talking nonsense

Our love of mobile phones is costing us a lot of money: each of us is paying nearly €200 more a year for talking on them than everyone else in the EU. The average revenue per user across the Irish networks in the second quarter of this year was €44.07 per month, while the average across the EU was €29.40.

The mobile companies like to say, 'Ah, sure, isn't it because we have the gift of the gab and love to talk?' Actually, no, it's not. The French, for example, spend more time talking on their phones than we do but still end up spending only €34.66 on them every month.

Bad medicine

What's the story with the high retail prices we're asked to pay for both over-the-counter and prescription medicines? Some everyday drugs, such as low-dose aspirin and antibiotics, can cost as much as 75 percent less in Spain or the US than they do in the Republic. The pharmacists, the drugs manufacturers and the government all say that the higher prices are nothing to do with them, while consumers are left with no option but to cough up.

There are things you can do to avoid spending so much on medicine, such as stocking up on drugs when you're overseas or using the Internet to buy them, but as I have absolutely no medical qualifications – and no clue what's wrong with you – I'm not going to recommend either of these options. (I will say that once, when writing an article for the *Irish Times* about the ease with which you could obtain serious prescription meds online with no doctor's consultation, I ordered a month's supply of a particularly controversial anti-depressant. The article appeared on the day the drugs were, completely coincidentally, impounded by the scary Drugs Enforcement Board, which neatly disproved the central thesis of my article, namely that any old eejit could import any old drug because no one was watching!)

Something borrowed, something blue

While a perfectly lavish wedding can be hosted in Spain or Barbados for less than €10,000, the average Irish one costs three times that amount. This is hardly surprising when hotels force couples to buy wedding cakes at vastly inflated prices and then charge rental fees for the cake stand and the knife used to cut the damned thing. Then there are the 'wedding taxes', which automatically add 20 or 30 percent on to the cost of the flowers, transport, clothes, wines, food and almost anything else associated with the ceremony.

Bah humbug

Not wanting to be a killjoy or anything, but Christmas in Ireland might be the biggest rip-off of the lot. It costs at least twice as much here as it does in other EU countries, according to a study published last year. The average household spend on all the jolliness was found to be €1,399, double the EU average, and even that may be an underestimate. With some stores putting up their Christmas displays in September, nearly a third of the year is now spent extracting money from people in the name of good cheer.

The tipping point

Do not feel that you absolutely have to tip. We have gone from a nation which never tipped to one which, anxious to show that we are not mean, tips too extravagantly. For most people, the waiting staff are guaranteed a tip of more than 10 percent unless they actually spit in the soup right in front you while punching your partner on the nose. It should not be like this. If waiting staff are surly, unhelpful, incompetent or sloppy, then feck them, don't leave them anything

– and I say this as a person who waited tables in the early 1990s and was surly, unhelpful, incompetent and sloppy and didn't get left anything. By refusing to tip when service is bad, you can knock at least 10 percent off your restaurant bill. In fact, you might want to re-examine your whole attitude to tipping. Earlier this year, the *Irish Times* carried a little guide to tipping. The figures that were deemed acceptable are given in the table below.

Now maybe I'm mean (actually, I'm not) but I have a

Irish Times Guide to Tipping

Waiter: 10 to 15 percent of the bill
Barman: Discretionary, but a safe guide is the price of a drink at the end of a night   **Lounge staff:** A euro or two per round
Hairstylist: €5 to €10 per cut
Hair-dressing assistant: Around €2   **Beauty therapist:** Around €2
Hotel cleaning staff: €5 a night   **Postman:** €20 at Christmas
Refuse collector: €20 at Christmas

few issues with this list. I'm not going to buy a barman who studiously ignored me for what seemed like hours before grumpily taking my order and dumping my change in a large pool of Guinness he had thoughtfully poured out of my pint a drink at the beginning, middle or end of the night. Lounge staff, on the other hand, do deserve a tip, but €2 a round?

Hairstylists charging ridiculous amounts for cutting your hair and then looking for another tenner of top of that is just silly and can be dismissed. Ditto the hair-dressing assistant – although it sounds like they're earning peanuts, so they probably deserve your money more than the stylist. Giving the cleaning staff in a hotel a fiver a night is fine if you're staying for just one night, but if you're staying for a fortnight, you might as well take them out for dinner in the hotel on the night before you leave: it'd work out cheaper.

At the risk of never getting my post delivered again, I don't think my State-employed postman deserves twenty quid from me at Christmas, or at any other time of the year, for simply slipping the occasional bill through my letterbox. Now if he actually delivered those parcels that I ordered from Amazon instead of posting a form through my door claiming he tried to do so but couldn't because I wasn't home when I clearly was, he might get something.

The bin men get nothing from me either, which is an arrangement we have had in place for many years, and we both seem happy with it. They don't come knocking looking for money, and if they did, I'd tell them to sling their hook. Actually, that's a complete lie. I'd hide under the duvet and pretend I wasn't home until they left.

This is not to suggest that you be mean – a pretty objectionable personality trait – but by refusing to tip automatically you make the point that you are not going to be taken for a mug by anyone any longer.

Make-up for less

Make-up costs a fair whack, but there are ways to make small savings. If you return six empty MAC plastic containers, you'll get a free lipstick worth approximately €20, which is not to be sneezed at. If you buy a Body Shop discount card for €10, you will receive a gift worth over €10 on your birthday, plus additional gifts worth over €10 and €15 when you collect four loyalty stamps, as well as 10 percent off every purchase. All told, it adds up to quite a good deal. And when it comes to buying all brands of cosmetics, it pays to shop around online. Websites like Strawberry.net and BeautyFlash.co.uk offer expensive skin-care products and cosmetics at very reduced rates. Generally speaking, however, products are shipped directly from Hong Kong, the USA and other countries outside the EU, so watch out for additional VAT charges.

Total savings this month: €100 (and that's just by being smarter with your credit cards)

Month 5

The savings that can be made by being savvy about how you manage the various insurance products you take out – both those which you are obliged to get by either the State or a mortgage company, or those policies you take out for your own peace of mind – put all other potential savings in the ha'penny place. Generally speaking, car, home and house insurance policies have to be renewed annually, and insurance companies or brokers have to send out renewal notices at least fifteen days before the renewal date. These notices (particularly those from brokers) will say that they have done all the shopping around on your behalf and found that your existing policy is the most competitive. Don't listen to them: they might be lying. Not all of them, perhaps – there are some very honest and genuinely helpful insurance brokers out there – but most of them. Finding cheaper insurance than you already have is perhaps the easiest and most profitable – if admittedly one of the dullest – ways to spend an afternoon.

Now you're motoring

Unlike pretty much everything else that you're likely to spend money on, motor-insurance premiums have fallen significantly in recent years. In fact, canny and careful drivers should have seen the cost of their policies fall by as much as 50 percent over the last five years. A number of factors have led to this unexpected but most welcome development. The setting up of the Personal Injuries Assessment Board (PIAB) in 2003, which reduced legal costs for insurance companies, is one, and an improvement in the road-safety environment – such as the roll-out of the penalty-points system and the introduction of random breath testing – is another. However, it's the increased competition between new players in the market (who saw the profits that were to be had in this market) and existing insurers fiercely determined to hang on to their customer base that has seen consumers really benefit.

But the insurance companies are never going to come cap in hand to you offering you the substantial discounts which are now commonly available; you have to go looking for them.

Unlike health insurance, which is optional, motor insurance is a legal requirement. The levels of cover available are fairly limited, and broadly similar from company to company. More than any other insurance package, the single biggest driver of how you choose your motor insurance should be price.

Quotes can differ wildly. According to a recent survey from our hard-working friends at the Financial Regulator, a twenty-two-year-old male driver of a modified Honda Civic from County Clare (the driver, that is, not the car – that comes from Japan) can save up to €3,875 a year on his car-insurance premiums if he shops around.

While you might not be able to make such substantial savings (unless you happen to be a twenty-two-year-old Clare man driving a modified Honda Civic, it's still worth making a few calls before your next renewal date. And if you do get a lower quote, make sure that you let your current company know all about it: you'd be amazed at how often they'll match your new quote simply in order to hang on to your business.

Home free (well, almost)

Just before Christmas, a colleague of mine managed to save herself a thousand euro on her mortgage-tied life-assurance policy by making three phone calls. She had a policy with a major bank which was costing her and her husband €109 a month. The insurance policy had been taken out at the same time as the mortgage had been drawn down, so it seemed like a comparatively small amount. Months later, she realised that charging a non-smoking couple in their early thirties €1,308 a year in life insurance which would only clear the mortgage on their property in the event of one of them dying and would not pay out millions of euro with which to furnish a lavish lifestyle made no sense, so she decided to shop around. Within minutes, the website 123.ie had found her a joint policy with a price tag of €639 per year with a 50 percent discount in year one. Even if she just switched for a single year, she'd save herself more than €900; over the lifetime of her mortgage, her savings would amount to €13,700. Is it any wonder that the big banks are (or at least were, before last year's credit crunch gave them a bloody nose) able to report such staggering profits year in, year out?

Home-insurance prices at a glance

Alliance €283	Axa €211	Eagle Star €320
FBD €283	Quinn Direct €238	Royal & Sun Alliance €206

All prices quoted covered a three-bedroom terraced house in Dublin 5 with a rebuilding cost of €210,000 and contents valued at €30,000.

Travel safely

Not only is travel insurance almost certainly the dullest thing on any summer-holiday checklist, it is also considered by many people to be a complete waste of money, thanks to some unscrupulous tour operators, who zealously flog over-priced policies to unwitting holidaymakers.

But once you look beyond the boredom and the sharks, it probably should be the first thing in your suitcase. If something goes wrong while you're on holidays this year and you're one of the 40 percent of Irish people who don't have insurance, the oversight could end up costing you an arm and a leg.

With all manner of terrible things – including cancelled flights, lost bags, theft, illness, wars, earthquakes or worse – just waiting to happen, it is remarkable that nearly half of us blithely disregard the gods and go on holiday without bothering to take out any insurance at all. (According to a recent study, only 57 percent of Irish people who travelled abroad for leisure purposes in 2006 had insurance.)

With travel insurance, the cheapest option is not always the best one: what is of far greater importance is an understanding of the terms and conditions which govern the policy. These terms and conditions can extend to more than twenty-five pages of densely written prose which most people don't bother with.

You should also be wary of any travel insurance offered in conjunction with your credit card, no matter how attractive the issuer makes it seem. While I don't like to use the word 'useless' often, this form of insurance is, generally speaking, just that. Often, when you study the terms and conditions, you're only being offered fairly limited accident insurance covering incidents which occur while you are on a train, bus, plane or

rented car which has been paid
for using the card: not much use
when you find you've been bitten
by a Portuguese man-of-war
while diving in the Caribbean.

Travel-insurance prices at a glance

AIB Single trip €41 Multi-trip €81

Bank of Ireland Single Trip €50 Multi-trip €107

123.ie Single Trip €35 Multi-trip €76

AA Single trip €28 (members) €35 (non-members) Multi-trip
€115 (members) €145 (non-members)

VHI Single trip N/A Multi-trip €49 (available to members only)

ACE Single trip €18 Multi-trip €49

GetCover Single Trip €45 Multi-trip €69

All prices are for worldwide travel insurance for one person; the
single-trip polices are for up to seventeen days, and the multi-
trip policies are for up to one year.

Dos and don'ts for a happy holiday

• *Do* arrange your travel insurance well in advance. Some 65 percent of all claims are for cancellations due to changing circumstances or family bereavements.

• *Do* read the terms and conditions. Yes, it is tiresome, and you sometimes need a microscope to read the fine print, but there's no point in buying a policy only to find that it's invalidated because of that whitewater-rafting incident.

• *Do* bring all emergency contact details with you even if you're going on a package holiday. Unless you have taken a policy out directly with a tour operator, the reps won't have a breeze about what you need to do to make an emergency claim.

• *Do* keep all your receipts. If you incur any expenses because of lost baggage, crime or illness, your claim will not be entertained unless you can actually prove you bought that Picasso etching.

and the Don'ts....

• *Don't* forget to contact the local police in the event of a theft overseas. In the absence of a police report, a claim will be difficult or impossible to make successfully.

• *Don't* forget to sign up for a European Health Insurance Card if you're travelling within the EU. This is not a replacement for travel insurance and won't cover repatriation costs or lost money, baggage or cancellations, but it's useful all the same. Forms can be downloaded from www.ehic.ie/onlineapp.htm. And don't just download the form: fill it in before going on holiday.

Phone it in

Mobile phones are stolen every couple of minutes in Ireland, the mobile phone companies like to warn us. And if they're not being thieved, they are being lost in the pub or dropped in the bath – which is why we should be eternally grateful for the peace of mind we get from the insurance policies we are artfully persuaded to take out when we buy a new model.

Or maybe we're just being conned into buying products which have little or no value and are just another example of big business making money out of consumers while purporting to act in their best interests.

Many aspects of the mobile-phone insurance business suggest that it is the latter. The profits companies make are pretty shocking, for a start. If the policy covering an ordinary handset costs you €6 a month, you will probably pay out more than half the value of the phone in insurance every year. So, for your policy to make any financial sense, you'd need to make a claim every two years – more frequently if you factor in the excesses all companies attach. It's a bit like paying €200,000 a year to insure a house that's worth €400,000.

And it's not just the relative cost to value that raises eyebrows. When it comes to mobile-phone insurance, there are so many restrictions that it is hard to conclude that the policy is not a waste of money, particularly when replacement handsets are so cheap. A look at the terms and conditions shows excesses starting at €31.74. Once you have made one claim, the excess increases to €75, making the value of the policy even more open to question. And if you're unlucky enough to lose your phone a third time in a twelve-month period, you can forget about reclaiming anything.

If your phone is lost or stolen, and you don't have insurance, you might find yourself being quoted an outlandish price to have the handset replaced. Don't pay it. Rather than shelling out unquestioningly, it might be worth considering switching networks. You get to keep your number and will probably be offered some class of deal sweetener by the new operator. And you get to teach your old operator a lesson.

Total savings this month: €600

▶ Month 6

Check out before you check in

If you're not crazy enough to queue up overnight in the depths of the winter sales for a cheap sun holiday, as some people seem to do every year, but still don't want your break to cost the earth, there are ways you can take excellent holidays for half-nothing.

There was a time when we were all in thrall to our travel agents. We'd queue in the offices at the start of the year, give our requirements to the person behind the counter, and watch in bemusement as they typed Lord-only-knows-what at incredible speeds into a computer before pointing at a couple of tiny pictures in a brochure and suggesting that X, Y or Z might be suitable. Then you'd pay your deposit and away you'd go, having placed considerable trust in the travel agent. It's all changed now, of course, and by doing your research online you can get a much clearer understanding of what you're getting, including video tours of hotels, 360-degree images, and pages and pages of customer feedback covering almost every resort on the planet. If you book online, there's a good chance you'll get a much better deal too.

With airlines taking Web-only bookings, hoteliers using their own home pages to sell directly to tourists, and online travel services such as Lastminute.com offering low-cost packages, the world can be your low-cost oyster. Earlier this year, a travel agent in Dublin was offering weekend breaks in Barcelona for €319. The deal covered flights and two nights' accommodation in a three-star hotel in the coolest of city centres. After less than ten minutes online, a virtually identical package was found for €292 – not a huge saving but a saving nonetheless.

People planning a DIY holiday to an unfamiliar destination can end up at the wrong airport and find themselves five hours from their accommodation, late at night, when the trains and buses have stopped running and the car-hire company has closed. This might not appeal to everyone (or indeed anyone), so common sense will be required, and fall-back positions should be researched just in case everything does indeed go wrong.

TripAdvisor is the second-biggest travel website, after hotel-, flights- and car-booking service Expedia, and the biggest online destination for travel information and advice. The site, which gets 20 million visitors a month, is based on a brilliantly simple concept: users are invited to post their unvarnished impressions of the accommodation they have used. The site features more than 4 million travel reviews and opinions, allowing tourists to check out, sometimes in great detail, what to expect before they check in.

The timing of your holiday is also crucial if you don't want it to cost the earth. People without children of school-going age should never, ever book their holidays for the months of June, July and August. Demand is at its peak during these months, so prices are, obviously enough, vastly inflated. Earlier this year, a two-week holiday in the Cretan resort of Stalis for two adults in the first two weeks of July with Budget Travel would have cost me €709 per person. Not bad. Until you compare it to the cost of a two-week break booked with the same operator in the same complex in the same Cretan resort in the *second* two weeks of May: €497. By juggling the dates, I made a saving of €212. Having been in Crete in both May and July, I can tell you that it is infinitely more pleasant in May – and the rather splendid water park not far from that particular resort is a lot quieter too. So if it doesn't matter to you when you take your holiday, take your breaks in May or September: anything else is just plain silliness.

A home away from home

While house-swapping might not be for everyone, it is certainly a route which offers incredible savings to people who are fortunate enough to live in a house, and in a location, which people from other countries might find even slightly desirable. One man who featured on RTÉ's *Highly Recommended* consumer show, on which I was a judge, claims to have saved himself in the region of £25,000 over the last twenty years by swapping his home in Northern Ireland with people from across Europe and the United States. Not only does this approach save money on holidays, it saves on car hire as well. I'm not sure how practical it is for some people, though. Some people would not be able to relax in a stranger's house and might be even more concerned about strangers staying in their house. The level of cleaning required is considerably greater than it would be if you were staying in a hotel, the fear of breaking something might stress some people out, and then there's the problem of finding someone to swap houses with you if you live in a prefab on a particularly windswept stretch of the M50. But it's certainly worth considering. Here are a few websites showing you what's on offer when it comes to swapping homes, and what kind of savings you can make:

houseswap.ie
homeexchange.com
homelink.ie

Total savings this month: €200

The big screen

Cinema tickets aside, savings that can be made on your trips to the movies. Stock up on treats before you go, as cinema foyers are no place to buy your soft drinks, chewing gum and sweets. A small bottle of mineral water will cost you €2.50 in the foyer – and even more in some cinemas, if you can believe it – while exactly the same bottle of water in the local shop next to the cinema will cost half that. And no cinema I have ever come across objects if you bring your own refreshments in. Although I don't think that stretches to a curry and a flagon of cider.

Keep an eye out for special deals and membership cards which can save significant sums. Take, for example, CineWorld on Dublin's Parnell Street. It has an 'Unlimited Card', which gives you access to the cinema for just €19.99 a month – compared with a single-ticket price of just under €10.

Total savings this month: €200

Month 7

Phone calls for less

We moan about high phone charges, but we really only have ourselves to blame for how much we spend on calls. There is a world of free (and dirt-cheap) phone calls available to anyone who has broadband access and a computer.

Despite the fact that the Internet offers simple ways to circumvent the sometimes ridiculous costs imposed by telecommunications companies for line rental, calls to mobiles, and long-distance calls, most of us continue to turn our backs on the money-saving technology: a recent trends survey showed that less than half of Irish people polled had even heard of Voice over Internet Protocol (VoIP), never mind used it.

The survey found that just 17 percent of those polled had used Skype or a similar Internet telephony service. More surprising still, when asked whether they would consider using the Internet in the future to make voice calls, 52 percent said no.

This reluctance is a little surprising, given the ease with which the Internet can be used to make calls. VoIP works along the same principles as e-mail, and all users need is a software programme that creates a virtual phone-dial panel on a computer. This panel can then be used to dial other computers that have the same software – which can be installed for free – as well as landlines and mobiles anywhere in the world at a very small cost.

The process is simple, even for the most chronic technophobe, and can be completed in minutes. When the software has been installed, you just log in and start dialling.

It's free to call Skype to Skype, but if you want to call a landline or a mobile phone from your computer, you need to buy call credit, which can be done at the Skype website. Calls to regular landlines are currently 2 cent a minute to Australia, the US and Britain, while calls made to mobiles, in Australia for example, cost in the region of 1.5 cent a minute.

Its low cost and ease of use has turned Skype into a global phenomenon. Its user base has increased from 40 million to nearly 200 million since eBay paid $2.6 billion for the company in September 2005.

Blueface is the leading residential VoIP service in Ireland, with a growing number of subscribers. For around €15 a month, it offers unlimited calls to Irish and UK landlines, and for €25 per month you get unlimited calls to 'most of the

industrialised world', as the Blueface people put it on their website.

Internet telephony has more serious disadvantages than the occasional disconnected call, however. Spammers and scammers are eager to target the sector in the same way that they pollute e-mail communication, and security experts are certain that this problem will grow as more VoIP systems come on line. Some Internet-service providers impose limits on how much data a user can download, and Internet telephony can make short work of lower limits: three or four hours' worth of calls weekly might be all you get before you exceed the limit. There are also question marks over how reliable this system is in an emergency. For a start, it can prove immensely difficult to trace a call made using Skype, and in a power cut VoIP networks go down, unlike regular phone networks.

VoIP providers worth checking out:

blueface.ie
freespeech.ie
skype.com

If you make a lot of long-distance phone calls and don't fancy going down the Internet-telephony route, then make sure you use phone cards rather than just dialling from your landline. There are approximately fifty million prepaid call cards sold in Ireland annually. The card providers buy vast amounts of 'bulk minutes' to provide the customer with significant savings when making calls. Make sure only to buy cards from recognised operators, however, as there are rogue operators in the market just waiting to rip people off.

And then there's the subject of mobile-phone costs. According to an alarming study of people's mobile-phone habits which was published recently, we may be to blame for a significant portion of our inflated bills, and if we were just a little cuter we could save a bundle.

The online survey, carried out by British price-comparison website **moneysupermarket.com**, found that confusion over phone tariffs in the UK could be costing Britain's sixty-five million phone users a colossal £8bn a year. It said that many phone users were completely clueless about how many free minutes or free text messages were included in the phone packages they had, or even how long they spent talking and texting each month.

The study reported that such ignorance was costing customers as much as £130 each per year. With many of the same mobile-phone operators doing business here, similar confusion could be costing Irish phones users tens of millions of euro annually.

Phone users on the state's biggest network, Vodafone, spent an average of just over €45 per month in the second quarter of last year – well above Vodafone's European average, incidentally. The mobile-phone giant's Irish customers spoke, on average, for 234 minutes and sent 120 text messages compared to a European average of 146 minutes and 63 messages.

By signing up to the company's Perfect Choice 100 package, users get 100 free minutes and 100 free text messages for a very reasonable-looking €29 per month. If, however, they are the average Vodafone customer and make 234 minutes worth of calls and 120 texts, the additional charges of 30 cent per minute outside their bundled allowance would increase their monthly bill by €42.40 to €71.40.

If they switched to the Perfect Choice 200, which gives 200 free minutes and text messages at a cost of €49, and once again spoke for the average of 234 minutes, their final monthly bill would be just €57.50.

In the third quarter of last year, O2's average revenue per user was €47, while the average number of minutes used was 250 per month. Prepay customers paid a lot less – €29.20, compared with a monthly spend by contract customers of €84.90.

A contract customer signing up to O2's most popular bundled service, the Active Life 150 package, gets 150 free minutes and 100 texts at a cost of €35 per month. But if they talked for the O2 average, it would end up costing them an additional €45, taking their total monthly bill to €80. An Active Life 250 package, which, not surprisingly, gives 250 free minutes, costs just €50.

Free calls at weekends and to designated numbers further complicate matters and lessen the impact of being on the wrong tariff. Nonetheless, keeping an eye on your bills and going for that mobile-phone health check regularly is still a smart move.

Go pay as you go

In order to reduce your bills, you should first look at your usage and ask whether you really need all those 'free' minutes and 'free' text messages your provider offers you. If your mobile bill is around €60 a month, then it is costing you the guts of €700 each year. Do the maths, and if you're only a casual user, switch to a pay-as-you-go option – the handsets can be picked up for €30, including €10 of call credit – and save yourself hundreds of euro this, and every, year.

STOP WASTING YOUR MONEY

Taxing times

Given the regular fare increases we are faced with, it is hard to cut the cost of your commute, but there are certainly a couple of avenues worth exploring. The TaxSaver Commuter Ticket scheme operated by Dublin Bus and Iarnród Éireann in conjunction with the Revenue Commissioners was set up nearly ten years ago as an incentive for employees to use public transport. It involves employers providing employees with bus and rail commuter tickets, while saving on employer PRSI payments. Employees participating in the scheme benefit from reduced tax and PRSI payments of up to 47 percent. Employees receive tickets either as part of their salary package, known by the Revenue as 'salary sacrifice' or in lieu of an annual bonus. Savings arise because tickets are not subject to tax or PRSI.

Have a nice Weekender

Another way in which regular InterCity train users can cut costs is through the Weekender fare card offered by Irish Rail to all train users aged over twenty-six. (A similar system is in place for those under twenty-six.) This could save you a packet. A regular return ticket from Dublin to Galway costs a hefty €40, but the price falls to €25.50 if your ticket is bought with a Weekender fare card. The Weekender card allows rail users to travel the first leg of their journey on a Friday, Saturday or Sunday and use the return ticket no later than the following Tuesday.

The cost of the Weekender, which is valid for one year after the date of purchase, is €7, so even if you use it just the once, you're saving a fiver on the cost of a return ticket to the west (the savings vary depending on the route). Use the card to buy a rail ticket to Galway once a month, and you'll save nearly €160 in a year.

You'd imagine that such a good discount offer would be promoted very heavily by Irish Rail. Not a bit of it: it is actually very hard to find any information about it, anywhere. The only thing to remember is that you'll need to have a passport photograph about your person when buying your first Weekender card. Irish Rail staff will happily take their scissors to your expired card and recycle your picture from then on in.

Hair raising

When it comes to hair, the best money-saving tip I can think of – by an enormous margin – is to shave it off completely. That's what I did ten years ago, and I reckon I've saved the guts of a thousand euro since then on shampoo, trips to the barbers and hair gel – not to mention the stress of watching it fall out of its own accord! I accept that this might not be a tip that'll work for everyone, so I've tried to come up with at least one way to reduce the cost of getting your hair done.

Just looking at the prices some of the fanciest salons charge would make your hair fall out. I'm told by a reliable (female) source that spending in excess of €150 on a haircut is not uncommon. The same source tells me that the only way to make considerable savings is to turn your back on the trendy city-centre places in favour of the local salons in your locality. By getting your hair done locally, you can easily knock €100 of the cost of a visit; this is also the best way of guaranteeing that you get the same stylist to look after you time and time again.

Another way to get yourself a cheaper haircut is to check out the local hairdressing schools in your area. There are loads of them about the place, and they are always looking for models – though bear in mind that this is not something you should really consider if you're getting some class of elaborate hairdo. But for a simple cut and blow dry, you can't really go wrong. And if it all goes pear-shaped, your hair will grow back.

Total savings this month: €150

Month 8

Seeing bargains clearly

Having poor eyesight costs you money. Just how expensive it can be became clear recently after a survey published in Britain found that the average glasses wearer there spends more than £200 (€296) a year on frames, lenses and eye care, while those with contact lenses can expect to pay closer to £600 (€888) when check-ups, lenses, solution, and back-up glasses are factored in.

These products and services are even more costly in Ireland, but there is one way that the short-sighted with foresight can make dramatic savings: by shopping around online. Buying glasses on the Internet, while possible, is problematic, as it is next-to-impossible to gauge how a pair will look without trying them on. With contact lenses, there are no such restrictions, and it has grown into a big online business.

On the Specsavers website, a six-month supply of all-day all-night lenses from Ciba Vision costs €155. On the VHI website, **vhi.ie**, bigger savings are to be found, and the same quantity of lenses of the same brand costs just €125. But it is by taking your business overseas that the real bargains can be made. One US-based website, **aclens.com**, is selling a six-month supply of the same Cibe Vision lenses for just €91, including delivery to Ireland.

With prices like these, is it any wonder that Irish consumers who have their eyes on a bargain are starting to take their business online? There can be risks involved in buying lenses from overseas, however. Many online providers of lenses who are selling into Ireland are not based in Ireland and therefore not subject to the same regulations as Irish opticians. This can cause significant concerns regarding patient safety and it does place significantly more responsibility on consumers to make sure that they look after themselves.

For people who do decide to buy lenses from companies based outside this jurisdiction, it is absolutely essential to have regular check-ups – at least once a year – to ensure that your prescription is up to date and your eyes remain healthy. Specsavers insists that users of its extended-wear lenses have a check-up every six months, which it provides free.

With any online supplier, you will need your prescription details: Irish websites require that you fax or e-mail scanned copies of the actual prescription to them before they will issue the lenses, while international sites have a more relaxed (and, critics say, less responsible) approach and simply need the information.

You should be able to get a copy of your prescription from your optician. When sending on the details, you will be asked to choose from a number of options. Typically, this might be the base curve (the curvature of your eye), and the diameter and power of the lens that you need.

Globally, there are only a handful of manufacturers of contact lenses. Boots's daily disposable lenses, for example, are made by Bausch & Lomb. Identical lenses can be found at widely differing prices depending on the brand, so if you find the cheapest brand you can save a fortune, without compromising the quality – assuming, of course, that they are suitable.

When buying lenses, it is also important to bear in mind that the larger the supply you buy, the cheaper it is. Purchasing three, six or preferably twelve months' supply is common, although you should not buy more than a year's supply in case your prescription changes. On the VHI website, most users opt for the three-month option.

The VHI site insists that orders will be dispatched only upon receipt of a contact-lens prescription which has been issued within the past twelve months, and it will supply only enough lenses to last the duration of the prescription.

While international sites allow shoppers to circumvent this rule, this is not something that should be considered, as the cost of damaging your vision in the search for cheaper lenses would of course be far greater than the savings that can be made.

Claim what's yours

Are you claiming all the money that is your due back from the tax man? Do you know what you're entitled to claim back, or how to go about finding out about it? It's all too easy to miss out on tax relief which you might be due because you fail to claim what's yours. Medical expenses, dental costs, local-authority charges, employment expenses, union dues and rent relief are just some of the tax reliefs that routinely go unclaimed by PAYE workers. The first place to start looking is the Revenue Commissioners' website, **revenue.ie**. Unfortunately, this is not a particularly user-friendly website, and some of the material is so incomprehensible that hundreds of euro that you could be getting back might go unclaimed just because you can't find your way around the site. So if you're in any doubt, make sure to call them and ask – while the

website may be hard to follow, the staff are surprisingly helpful!

If you pay union dues, you can get tax relief. Ditto on your mortgage, your rent, certain health and dental expenses, and some prescription drugs. When it comes to prescription drugs, you should be paying the first €85 per month of your costs; the State pays the rest. Anything that's not refunded can be claimed as a tax relief. If you pay tax at 20 percent and have allowable medical expenses of €1,000, for instance, then you are entitled to claim €200 back; if you pay tax at 41 percent, your refund will be €410.

Flat-rate employment expenses are one of the Revenue's hidden gems. To quote the Revenue, these are 'expenses that are incurred in the performance of the duties of the employment and are directly related to the nature of the employee's employment'. A standard flat-rate expenses allowance is set for various classes of employee. For example, airline cabin crews are granted flat-rate expenses of €64 per annum, while teachers get between €518 and €608 every year. The amount of the deduction is agreed between Revenue and representatives of groups or classes of employees. (The employees are usually represented by trade-union officials.) The agreed deduction is then applied to all employees of the class or group in question.

The bad news is that you have to apply for this relief; the good news is that the amount claimed can be backdated. When I was first told by my wife that journalists could claim something like €158 a year, I didn't really believe it. 'How could it be that all this money was just waiting for me to come get it,' I thought. Still, I called the Revenue and after a phone conversation that lasted less than three minutes all the paperwork had been done. Weeks later, I received an expenses cheque from the Revenue backdated over five years for in excess of €700.

A full list of the professions which can claim an expenses allowance can be found here: **http://www.revenue.ie/services/flat_rate_exps.xls**

Ten other areas of relief

- Rent-a-room relief
- Rent relief for private rented accommodation
- Tax relief for loan interest (secured and unsecured)
- Medical-insurance premiums
- Home carer's tax credit • Trade-union subscriptions
- Tax relief on service charges
- Health/medical-expenses relief • Dental work • Tuition fees

Free at last

Microsoft owner Bill Gates did not become one of the world's wealthiest men by giving away his products for nothing. Microsoft and many other well-known, long-established software providers charge considerable amounts for their products and are perfectly within their rights to do so. By the same token, however, you are perfectly within your rights not to pay these sums and to go looking for similar software free somewhere else. There is a vast amount of high-quality, professional-level software legally available for free on the net, and it is no exaggeration to say that thousands of euro worth of free applications, including word-processing software, photograph and video software, and a wide range of office applications are out there with a price tag of nothing at all.

Tens of thousands of techies from all over the world spend much of their time contributing to developing free applications, partly out of altruism, and partly because they don't like Microsoft. There is freeware (which, surprisingly enough, is free), and shareware (which you can use for a certain period of time, after which an annoying message keeps popping up reminding you that the product isn't, strictly speaking, supposed to be free, and would you mind paying out a small amount for an upgrade?).

Microsoft Office software costs well over €100, while openoffice is a free and fully functioning suite of office programmes. It includes software which is comparable to MS Word, MS Excel, MS Powerpoint, and MS Access except for the price. It is also compatible with documents written in all those programmes.

Then there is the unfortunately named Gimp software, which is an almost perfect free replacement for the

considerably more expensive
Photoshop.

Two places to look for
free software

openoffice.org
download.com

Five things to do in Dublin instead of spending money

National Museum of Ireland: Archaeology and History, Kildare Street

This is where you can see pretty much all the important archaeological objects ever found in Ireland. The museum houses more than two million such artifacts, dating from between 7000 BC and the late-medieval period. The museum has the 'finest collection of prehistoric gold artefacts in western Europe, outstanding examples of metalwork from the Celtic Iron Age, as well as the Museum's world-renowned collection of medieval ecclesiastical objects and jewellery' and also 'houses a rich collection of Egyptian material and an historical exhibition which deals with the political background and events which culminated in the signing of the Anglo-Irish Treaty in 1921'. Not bad for free.

National Museum of Ireland: Decorative Arts & History, Collins Barracks

This museum, close to Heuston Station and on the Luas line, is home to a wide range of objects, including weaponry, furniture, silver, ceramics and glassware, as well as examples of folklife and costume.

The National Botanic Gardens, Glasnevin

A wonderful and – thankfully for those of us who visit it frequently – under-utilised resource in Dublin – that is extremely pleasant to visit any time of the year, except, of course, when it's raining, when it's pretty miserable, to be honest.

National Library of Ireland, Kildare Street

A vast selection of books, manuscripts, records, newspapers and maps are on show here, and it is certainly the place to visit if you fancy a spot of genealogical investigation.

Chester Beatty Library, Dublin Castle

The Chester Beatty Library is a gem of an art museum and library. It houses the great collection of manuscripts, miniature paintings, prints, drawings and rare books assembled by Sir Alfred Chester Beatty. Egyptian papyrus texts, beautifully illuminated copies of the Koran, the Bible and European medieval and Renaissance manuscripts are among the highlights of the collection.

Total savings this month: €350

Month 9

With electricity bills rising, and hardly likely to fall in the near (or even distant) future, it pays to be energy efficient. You could easily knock 25 percent off your electricity bill through a series of simple energy-saving measures.

Stay warm for less

The depths of winter is probably not the best time to be fooling around with your heating systems, so take action in a month when it's not so cold. Assuming that you haven't got solar panels in your roof, a wind farm in the garden, and acres of land to grow oats for bio-fuel, the steps you take to reduce your energy bill will be comparatively small, but effective way of saving hundreds of euro each year. Yes, you might have to wear that extra geansaí, as the ad has it, but the money you save will go some way towards funding your two weeks in the sun, when you can leave all your gansaís at home.

According to the Power of One campaign, which promotes energy efficiency at a personal and environmental level, families can save between €500 and €1,000 each year by making fairly small modifications to the way they heat and light their homes. Let's start with the heating. Turning down the thermostat by a single degree will knock 10 percent off your annual heating bill – and won't make a blind bit of difference to you.

The next thing you need to do is to shave a tiny amount off the time you have the heating on. Most families fall quite easily into a routine which sees their heating go on for a short time in the morning and then for a longer period in the evening.

The first step is to reassess how much heat you actually need to be comfortable. This is not to suggest that you sit shivering in your living room, wearing six jumpers and a duffle coat through the depths of the winter's cold snap. If done correctly, you shouldn't even notice the change.

Start off by reducing the amount of time the heating is programmed to come on by an hour at the end of the evening. If your rooms get too cold, then modify the timer so that it switches itself off forty minutes earlier, and see how you're fixed then. Keep playing with the time until you've reached a temperature that's comfortable for you. If you can reduce the time the heat is on by just 10 percent, that will obviously knock another 10 percent off your monthly heating bill – which could amount to another €100 in

your pocket over the course of a year.

Water, water everywhere

Back in the 1970s, immersion tanks were a national obsession, and there was no greater crime than leaving them on – especially on the 'bath' setting – even for a few minutes longer than was absolutely necessary. While no one wants to go back to the time when people's showers had to be timed with military precision, keeping an eye on the hot water is a way of significantly reducing your energy bill.

What you need to be aiming towards is reducing the time your spend unnecessarily heating hot water. Evaluate how much hot water you actually use, and set the lowest target possible for the length of time the immersion is on when the central heating is not in use. Obviously, prioritise use of the shower over the bath:

it is not only cheaper but also a great deal faster too. Wash dishes in a basin and not under a hot running tap. If the heating isn't on an immersion timer to heat the water from 6 PM until 7 PM each day, then turn it on for boosts as and when needed. Lastly, a lagging jacket on your water tank can save you €2.50 a week, or more than €120 a year.

A big turn-off

The average Irish family will spend up to €600 a year on electricity to power just five common appliances: the fridge, tumble dryer, washing machine, dishwasher and TV. The importance of the rating systems can not be overstated: an A-rated freezer will cost you 60 percent less to run than an old, G-rated version. So while running out and replacing every older piece of equipment you have might not be the best idea in the world, it is worth paying very close attention to the rating information when shopping for new appliances.

The simplest step you can take to stop wasting your money is to turn off electrical equipment when you're not using it. Yes, of course you've heard it a million times before, but it really needs to be done if you're serious about saving yourself a few bob – never mind saving the planet!

Standby mode is anathema for the sensible. TVs, PCs, printers, DVD players, PlayStations and toothbrush rechargers left in standby mode use 20 percent of the electricity they do when they're on full power – and you're paying for it.

Unplug chargers when not in use, and when your phones or laptop is fully recharged, plug them out. Switch off all unnecessary electrical equipment and appliances at night. Use the dishwasher only when it's absolutely full. If possible, make use of efficiency settings, e.g. reduced time/temperature settings when appropriate. Ditto with the washing machine, and try to use the 30-degree quick wash – unless your clothes are absolutely manky, of course. Minimise the use of the tumble dryer and hang your clothes outside when possible.

Does your fridge really have to be that cold? If cheese and eggs are freezing and icicles are forming on your lettuce leaves, then the answer is probably no. Even if it's not that cold, turn the setting up a notch. Boil only as much water in your kettle as you need. Think about your TV. We are in love with our flat-screen TVs and are second only to the British when it comes to buying the things. If you are considering buying one, bear in mind that an LCD TV is far more energy-efficient than a plasma one. The annual running cost of a Sony Bravia TV is around €30, while an MTV *Cribs*–style monster plasma model will cost in excess of €200 in electricity.

Turn off the lights in rooms you're not in, and switch to energy-efficient light bulbs. Compact fluorescent lights use 80 percent less power than ordinary bulbs and last fifteen times longer, so they are essential if you are serious about saving yourself a few bob. Apart from anything else, thanks to the good people in the Green Party, incandescent bulbs are set to be outlawed in this country within a year – although this might not happen quite as soon as Minister for the Environment John Gormley would like, as the government may be forbidden from enacting legislation banning products which are legally available in other EU member states.

Movies online

If you rent a lot of DVDs, you should certainly consider moving your business away from your local store and on to the Web. OK, you have to be a bit more organized, but it can work out substantially cheaper, and you won't have to leave your house in the driving rain to get a movie. Plus, you'll never be stung for late returns again. Renting a new-release DVD costs around €5 per night. If you rent more than two movies a month, consider signing up to an online service such as **moviesbymail**, from An Post, **Busybeedvd.ie**, **Moviestar.ie** or **Screenclick.com**, where a month's subscription costs from about €7.99 – although for that you only get a maximum of two DVDs each month.

Petrol Watch

Petrol prices vary enormously from forecourt to forecourt, so shop around. If you're too busy – or too lazy – to put in the legwork yourself, then check out **irishfuelprices.com**, where someone has probably done it for you. Or if you're even too lazy to check out the website, take it as read that your local Tesco will have the cheapest petrol in your locality: Tesco petrol stations are usually around 10 cent per litre cheaper than other garages in the area. It might not be worth driving long distances to get to the garage, but if you're going shopping anyway it pays to fill up there. Beware of false economies when it comes to petrol prices,

however. It makes no sense to drive miles out of your way and leave the engine running as you wait in line just to fill your tank with the cheapest petrol in your town. It would be much more economical to drive a little less to save a little less per litre.

Another tip to help you stay on top of your petrol costs is always to buy the same amount of petrol – as measured in litres, not euro. If you only ever buy 20 litres of petrol, then you will always be aware of the different prices at different petrol stations.

Find it for free

If you're in the market for free stuff, then look no further than Free Trade (**dublinwaste.ie**), the Dublin local authorities' online initiative which helps people pass on their unwanted household items for nothing. Everything from baby-changing stations to computer inks and three-piece suites is currently sitting there just waiting to find a new home. When I last had a look just before this book went to print, baby baths, toddlers' beds, buggies and sandpits were all available for free, as were DVD players, sofas and filing cabinets of various vintages.

While there is a lot of useless tat on the site, there are gems there too, and it's certainly worth a look; not only is it free, it's better for the environment than buying new products. Similarly, if you have stuff you don't want any more, register with the site and give it away. Apart from anything else, it'll reduce your refuse charges. If you're not in the Dublin area, then check out **freecycle.org** or **jumbletown.ie** for similar services in your area.

Total savings this month: €200

Convenience cons

Far too often, people throw their money away by not thinking about how much they are spending on the products they consume daily. There is a shop not far from where I work that sells cans of Coke for €1. The shop owner is perfectly entitled to sell soft drinks at any price he chooses – just as I am perfectly entitled not to buy them there. I've noticed that there is another shop, not fifteen metres from the first place, that sells cans of Coke for 70 cent. Yet every day, without thinking, people spend 30 cent more than they need to by going into Shop A rather than Shop B. The queues in both shops are identical, the range of stock is broadly similar, and the staff in both places are equally grumpy so there is nothing to distinguish the two outlets. Yet for some people, their Coke habit is costing them €70 more than it needs to every year.

Total savings this month: €200

Month 10

High prices, limited choice and the elbows and umbrellas of thousands of competing shoppers are the principal reasons why more Irish consumers than ever have turned their backs on traditional retailers and gone online in search of bargains. A recent survey from Deloitte showed that across the EU, Irish people are second only to the Germans when it comes to buying online. The survey reported that more than a third of shoppers used the Web as a source of cheaper gifts last Christmas, with a further quarter relying on it for research and to compare prices.

These price comparisons never make for comfortable reading for old-style retailers, with Christmas stocking fillers including CDs, DVDs, books and cameras routinely costing at least 20 percent less online – even when delivery charges are factored in.

High-street shops blame higher overheads here and differing tax regimes across the EU for the significant price disparities. And while they may have a point, should that really be of any concern to consumers who have grown tired of being bled dry? Of course not.

From the functionality and reliability of **Amazon.com** to the quirkiness and enormous potential to snag an amazing bargain of eBay, the Web has grown into a genuinely global marketplace – and one which people would be foolish not to exploit. Moreover, local retailers have taken to the Web and are passing on great savings to their customers as well.

Going, going . .

There is nothing like the auction website eBay for generating ridiculous marketplace tales. Not long ago, a pregnant Canadian recently attempted to sell the naming rights of her second child, as she had recently split from her husband and said she could not bear to name the child on her own. She might have done better to reduce the starting bid of $8,000 (€6,171), however, as the auction ended without a single bid being made. Then there was the Australian who posted his life for sale in 2007. The deal included his name, phone number, belongings, friends and potential lovers.

Stories such as these go a long way towards creating the impression that eBay is made up of oddballs selling ridiculous stuff to other oddballs. While there is certainly some truth in this, eBay did not grow into a €35 billion company in less than a decade by simply facilitating a trade in genial madness. With an Irish person reportedly buying something on the site every twenty seconds, it has become the first port of call for many canny consumers in search of everything from household furniture to computer equipment, baby buggies and vintage clothes.

Having bought an oak dining room table in the sales for €1,000, I was dismayed to learn that matching chairs would cost €300. That's €300 each. With a set of six costing almost double the price of the table, I decided to go online, where I found six solid-oak Victorian chairs in perfect condition. I bought the lot in an auction for €350. After adding the €150 delivery charge from the UK, the total was still €1,300 less than it would have cost to buy new chairs in Dublin. And they were delivered to my door nearly two months earlier than the department store could have managed.

It's not just in auctions that eBay bargains can be found. While the site is great for second-hand items, there is also good value in the millions of brand-new products populating its virtual shelves and selling for fixed 'buy it now' prices.

MP3 players and their accessories can be bought for half-nothing. iPod speakers which currently sell for more than €100 in Ireland can be bought and shipped from the Far East for a tenth of that price.

And a Canon digital SLR camera from the US currently has a 'buy it now' price of €693, similar to its cost in Ireland. However, the eBay deal also includes a tripod, an additional 70-300mm lens, extra memory and a camera bag, giving a total value of more than €500. This is very good value, even including the duty which Customs and Excise might slap on if your parcel is stopped and examined.

Although there are substantial savings to be made, it would be naive to suggest that shopping online is risk-free. Buying certain items, notably art, clothes and jewellery, sight unseen and with no physical contact either with the item or the seller, is obviously problematic. Taxes, when they are rigorously applied, and the charges imposed by delivery companies, which sometimes administer the taxes, can eat into the potential savings. Timely delivery is also a concern. In the run-up to Christmas, even the biggest online traders struggle to cope with the demand.

Then there is the spectre of fraud, which has cast a long shadow over Internet transactions. There are certainly risks involved in doing business on the Internet, and while tears of online identity theft and credit-card scams are dissipating, some people remain deeply suspicious when they are asked to leave their financial details on websites of uncertain provenance.

In that context, the European Consumer Centre's online tool aimed at helping consumers avoid online rip-offs is to be welcomed. The site, called 'Howard', gathers information on e-commerce websites, including when and where they were registered and whether they have 'trusted site' accreditation. By carrying out these rudimentary checks, consumers do not guarantee that their Internet transactions will always run smoothly, but they do give themselves another layer of protection from rogue traders, making the already attractive options available in the online realm even more secure.

Amazing Amazon

When it comes to buying books and CDs (if anyone still buys them any more), it is hard to top Amazon for choice and bargains – although **kennys.ie** is well worth a look for Irish-interest books, and **cd-wow.ie** is hard to top when it comes to CDs. Not long ago, researchers from British consumer group Which? filled a shopping basket with eight electrical items, including TVs and MP3 players, and found that by shopping online they could save more than £1,000 (€1,500). Even when delivery to Ireland is taken into account, things cost at least 20 percent less when they are bought online.

]

There is a but . . .

Unfortunately, **Amazon.co.uk** no longer delivers electronics goods to the Republic. The company says it is unable to deliver these items because of difficulties the site says it has encountered with the Waste Electronic and Electrical (WEE) recycling system in place here. When I queried its sudden decision to stop selling these goods to people in Ireland, a spokesman said the company had no option but to restrict the sale of electronic goods in order to ensure compliance with WEE recycling legislation. The spokesman assured us that the restrictions were temporary and said that Amazon was trying to find a resolution to the difficulty so that it could begin shipping electronics products to Ireland again.

Fair enough, we thought, until we noticed that computer software, PC and video games, and toys, games and video items which are neither electrical nor electronic were also not available to shoppers from the Republic. Nearly two years later, and the resolution I was led to believe was just around the corner is still nowhere to be seen.

Shop around

Some companies ship electronic goods to the Republic of Ireland at very competitive prices, including camera retailer **pixmania.com** and electronic retailers **dabs.com** and **komplett.ie**, while **cd-wow.ie** has long undercut traditional retailers when it comes to CDs. In addition to the savings that can be made and the convenience of shopping from your home (or office), buying online means that the websites can send the items directly to far-flung relatives and friends, saving you the bother of a trip to the post office.

It is worth remembering, however, that the prices quoted on the site may be misleading, as you still have to pay for shipping and, if you buy from outside the EU, you are liable for all taxes and duties in this country – as one reader found out to her cost. She recently bought some expensive skin-care products on a Hong Kong website and was delighted to get them at half the Irish prices. However, her parcel was opened by Customs, and when all the additional charges were taken into account, she saved only a few euro – hardly worth it, when you consider the delays and form-filling that was required.

Shopbots are your friend

By using a 'shopbot', you can find the cheapest prices online in less than a minute – and cut your online-shopping bill by as much as a third. The options available for buying a particular product online are dizzying, so there is a temptation to go to the same online retailer, like Amazon, over and over again. Shopbots – shopping robots – are sites for finding the cheapest prices for any product. One well-known shopbot **kelkoo.co.uk**. (Many of them are based in the UK.) When I searched the site for an 8 gigabyte iPod nano, it quickly drew up dozens of websites offering exactly the same product for anything between £110 and £140.

Five shopbots

kelkoo.co.uk

pricerunner.co.uk

checkaprice.com

pricegrabber.co.uk

bizrate.co.uk

Bought in the USA

The fact that the euro is extremely strong against the dollar at the moment makes buying from US-based websites even more attractive. While customs duty, VAT and delivery charges will eat into the savings, it still makes financial sense to check out the US sites first.

Call comparisons

One of the best services offered by the Communication Regulator ComReg is a price-comparison website that allows you compare the cost of the various deals from the mobile operators, the landline operators and the broadband operators. **callcosts.ie** is an invaluable resource that anyone who is concerned about their phone bills should check out. It is simple to use and easy to understand, and could prove invaluable when it comes to cutting through all the operator's marketing nonsense and advertising, and getting to the bottom line.

Total savings this month: €200

Month 11

Pre-owned

Anyone who is genuinely interested in saving will not need to be told that buying a new car is not the cleverest way to save yourself a few bob. Buying a good-quality second-hand car and taking care of it makes a lot more sense financially, and while it might sound unlikely, there is a way to get your hands on a top-of-the-range car for nothing, and it doesn't involve theft or being appointed to ministerial office. All it takes is a little research, a weekend away, and a fairly long road trip home, and you can drive for thousands of miles at little or no cost to yourself.

In fact, if you're really cute about it, you can actually make your car earn money instead of costing you a packet. The strategy for profitable motoring involves a short flight to London each year to visit Car Giant, one of the largest car showrooms in Europe. Cars costs up to €10,000 less there than they do in Ireland and, even after adding 20,000 miles, the cost of a few minor repairs, and crippling Vehicle Registration Tax (VRT), you might still be able to sell it a year later for almost exactly what you paid for it.

The number of imported vehicles coming into the country was 54 percent higher in the first quarter of 2007 compared with the same period in 2006, and 80,000 vehicles are likely to be imported in 2007.

A survey last year in the *Irish Times* Motoring supplement indicated that people keen on a car bargain do not even have to go as far as London, as there are plenty of great deals to be found north of the Border. A 2004 1.8-litre Toyota Avensis in Northern

Ireland worked out at 34 percent, or €7,238, cheaper than a virtually identical car in Galway, while €3,013 was saved on a 2004 Ford Focus 1.6 LX model compared to a similar car on sale in County Kerry. The saving on a 2004 Mercedes E220 CDI Classic was €10,433, while a 2004 Audi A4 1.9 TDI ended up costing €4,100 less in the North.

When you have decided on a make and model, it is obviously important to ensure that you are not being sold a lemon. London car dealers do not, it must be said, have the greatest reputation for honesty and decency in the world, so buyers should be wary. If you know a mechanic, bring them with you, or, more realistically, engage the services of the AA or the RAC in Britain to check the car out for you. It will cost a couple of hundred euro, but the peace of mind you get will make it money well spent. (One important caveat here is that some UK-registered cars which have been written off as dangerous and classed as not roadworthy following crashes have been sold to unsuspecting motorists in Ireland, so great care needs to be taken if pursuing this option.)

Download communism

'When you download music, you download communism' went the spoof poster, purporting to be from the Record Industry Association of America (RIAA) back in the last century, when the Internet was still regarded by many people as little more than a haven for hucksters and pornographers. Napster and Audiogalaxy had made free audio downloads easy to find, and record-industry executives and hard-rock drummers alike were trying to make sense of this appalling new vista, slapping lawsuits on anyone they could accuse of copyright theft.

Eventually, Napster was brought to heel and many of the other illegal download sites were shut down. It wasn't until Apple released the iPod that the download business stopped being a complete free-for-all and became, at least in part, a real business. And quite a profitable

one, too. In the UK alone, more than €1 billion worth of legally downloaded music is currently occupying space on computer hard drives. In 2007, almost 80 percent of the singles – 65 million – sold in the UK were downloaded legally from sites such as iTunes, which has a market share of more than 80 percent among digital-download sites. There were twice as many singles downloaded in 2007 as there were CD singles sold in 2005 – hardly surprising when you consider the price differential.

While a CD single costs in the region of €4 – for which price you also get the B-side and other material (which is often of dubious merit) – a song can be downloaded from iTunes for just 99 cent. This is not a lot to pay for a single. The price of a full album downloaded from iTunes is not quite such good value, however, particularly when you consider how little it costs to make the music available.

One country where MP3 prices have tumbled is Russia, where, to the consternation of record companies, music-download sites continue to thrive by massively undercutting the mainstream sites. First there was **allofmp3.com**, which sold albums for just over a euro a time, claiming that a loophole in Russian law allows it to sell the music legally, and ridiculously cheaply. The British Phonographic Institute (BPI) disagrees; it sued allofmp3, and eventually the site was shut down – for about fifteen minutes, before a new company, **legaldownloads.com**, set up shop in its place. Whether or not the site is legal is open to question, but it is certainly cheap.

There are a million places to look if you're in the market for free MP3s, so there's hardly any point in attempting to provide a comprehensive list here. One place I would recommend,

however, is the Internet archive **archive.org/details/etree**, if only to see the eclectic range of tunes on offer. It has a truly mind-boggling amount of music which is legally available to download for absolutely nothing at all. And I guarantee that you will have heard almost none of it before.

Read more (for free)

When was the last time you visited your local library? Back in the 1970s, when your parents dragged you kicking and screaming along to borrow a couple of Enid Blyton books every Saturday morning? Libraries are genuinely remarkable places that provide an amazing service which is terribly under-used by the reading public, who prefer to visit their local Eason's or Waterstones to hand over good money for blockbusters they'll read just once or cookbooks they'll browse through occasionally but rarely if ever cook from. Libraries are central, warm, pleasant, and above all else free.

Or if the library seems just a little old-fashioned, you could try something a bit cooler but almost as free. If you're anything like me, there are hundreds of books on your bookshelves – books that will almost certainly never be read again. Pick one of your favourites and register with the website **bookcrossing.com**. This is a free online book club that spans the globe. It has more than 300,000 members, sharing over 1.5 million books. When you register, you get an ID and the website address, which you stick on the book and give it to a friend, or leave it where someone is likely to pick it up and read it. Don't just dump it on the street, though: there's a fine line between sharing and littering. On the website, you can track the presence of your book and, importantly, get tips as to the location of other books which like-minded people have left about the place. When we last looked, four books had been left in Cineworld on Parnell Street in Dublin, another one in a branch of itsabagel, and three in Starbucks on Dame Street. Another user had left a book 'on Dawson Street' – which sounded just a little vague to me.

Saving the Earth (and a few bob) in ten easy steps

Where I live, we need to attach bin tags to our bins instead of using the more commonly found wheelie bins. The tags cost €2.50 a pop, and typically my family generates three binloads a week: that's €390 a year. This is on top of the recyclable rubbish, which is collected for nothing. If I can reduce the amount of household waste I produce by a third, which is no great stretch, I save myself €130 every year. If I can reduce it to a single bin bag each week – something which is easy to do given a little discipline – I'll save €260, which will cover a significant portion of a weekend in Paris for two every spring.

1. *Get a green cone* Partially buried in your garden, the solar-heated unit takes all cooked and uncooked food waste and breaks it down into its natural components. It can reduce household waste by about 25 percent, and costs €165. See **greencone.ie**.

2. *Have worms recycle and convert your organic rubbish into compost* Worms eat half their body weight daily. Remember, they require attention; otherwise, you'll be left with the blood of a thousand worms on your green fingers. A three-tray wormery costs about €150, while half a kilo of Tiger composting worms cost €30. See eco-ireland.com

3. *Cut down on packaging refuse by buying loose fruit and vegetables* Or better still, grow your own vegetables, raised on your own compost.

4. *Don't throw away old computers, phones or other electronic goods*
Try selling them on ebay.ie or donating them to charity. Many
dumped electrical goods still work, or need only basic repairs.
Companies such as Dell (dell.ie) run product-donation programmes.

5. *Don't dump bulky household goods* Sunflower Recycling operates
a collection service in inner-city Dublin. They'll take unwanted
furnishing, household and electrical goods for upgrade or recycling
at a cost of €30 for one item and €10 for subsequent items. Call 01
856 0251 or see **sunflowerrecycling.ie**

6. *Lobby banks and utility companies to stop sending paper bills in
favour of electronic versions*

7. *Flattening or squashing used packaging means you can fit more
into your recycling containers* Many stores sell funky devices to
facilitate the task.

8. *Make your own lunch instead of buying it* Not only will it reduce
refuse, it'll be nicer, better for you and save you more than a fiver a
day, or €1,200 a year.

9. *Put a 'no junk mail' sticker on your letter box* It will either reduce
your rubbish or alert you to companies who don't care what you
want.

10. *Remember, plastic is recyclable* True, not all kerbside collectors will accept plastic bottles for recycling, but you can locate your nearest plastic-bottle recycling facility at **repak.ie.**

Get yourself a gift cupboard

This takes organisation but if you can pull it off, the savings will be substantial. When you're out shopping and spot a promotional buy-one-get-one-free offer on something you think might make a nice present for some as-yet-unspecified person, buy it and put it in the cupboard. And if you get gifts which you have absolutely no use for, don't dump them, just put them in the cupboard. Do that for those presents your child gets but doesn't like or already has, and before you know it you will have a handy supply of emergency presents which you won't have had to pay over the odds for.

Pasta joke

One of the great cons of the last two decades must be jarred pasta sauces, which increase the size of your waistline while reducing the size of your wallet. Many of these sauces, which we've all lazily used on occasion, are filled with salt and sugar to make them taste vaguely nice. They are also ridiculously expensive. Let's say a 500g jar of a branded pasta sauce costs €2. (Some are cheaper than this, and some are much more expensive.) You buy it, add it to your mince, stir it about for a while and serve up a quick-and-easy – if not entirely wholesome – spaghetti Bolognese.

Now if, instead of doing all that, you chucked a can of tomatoes (€0.70) a diced onion (€0.15), a clove of garlic (€0.10) and some dried herbs (€0.05) into your minced meat, you'd have exactly the same dish – only much, much nicer, and much, much better for you – for half the price. And the only extra effort is chopping an onion and a piece of garlic – which will take you, what, a minute?

Total savings this month: €150

Month 12

Have yourself a black-bin party

I have to confess, I've never done this, but it sounds like a right old wheeze and is something I fully intend to do before the year is out. Get all your mates to put the clothes they no longer wear, the CDs they no longer listen to, the computer games they don't play any more, and any other stuff they have outgrown or lost interest in into black plastic bags and bring them round to your house. Then dump all the stuff into the centre of the room and allow everyone to have a good old rummage. The stuff that you've lost interest in may be just what someone else is looking for, and vice versa. Not only will you save money, and reduce the amount of material going into landfill, but you'll be able to laugh at each other's dreadful taste in clothes, music, games and books. I am told, however, that such parties are supposed to be contacted in an entirely non-judgmental fashion, so don't make too big a deal of it when your best pal produces a pair of sequined flares from the 1970s or a Marilyn Manson-style dog collar.

The price of celebrating

Celebrating Christmas in Ireland costs more than in any other EU country, according to a recent study. Research from Deloitte suggests that households here will spend, on average, €1,399 on the festive season – double the EU average. While this figure might seem like a lot, it is probably in fact somewhat wide of the mark. We broke Christmas down into twelve categories and found that, even by scrimping on food (we left the crisps, crackers and cake off our shopping list) and not going entirely mad partying and buying expensive wines and spirits to drink at home, it was hard to escape the season of goodwill for less than twice the estimated average.

1. Food

As Christmas approaches, Irish people tend to stock up on food as if they are heading into a nuclear winter – which might explain why we will consume around 6,000 calories each on Christmas Day and put on an average of half a stone. The Deloitte survey suggests that the average household spend on Christmas food is €251, but this figure may well be far too low. PriceWatch filled a virtual shopping trolley in Superquinn made up of a small turkey, ham, biscuits, mince pies, breakfast,

melon, plum pudding and a few other Christmas Day essentials. There was nothing in our basket that was out of the ordinary, and there were no high-end products either. The cost of our twenty-four items – enough to feed a family of five comfortably on the big day with a few leftovers for grazing on St Stephen's Day – came to a fairly hefty €255.08.

2. Drink

Not wanting to overdo it, we limited ourselves to a case of beer, four bottles of red wine, two bottles of fairly ordinary-looking champagne, a bottle of brandy for the lighting of the plum pudding and a bottle of whiskey, to make Irish coffees. The bill came to €173.91. Now add two adults going to the pub three times over the Christmas period and having four pints each on each occasion – hardly excessive by festive standards –

and the bill for alcohol rises to €300.

3. The christmas Party

While your company will hopefully fund your Christmas party – at least to some degree – it is unlikely to keep you in booze all night and will certainly not be paying for your taxi home. There might also be a Kris Kindle gift to factor in. We'll allow €30 for taxis, €30 more for drinks and another €10 for a gift for someone you don't know. So there's another €70 gone and, as there are two Christmas parties to go to in our imaginary home, let's double it.

4. The tree

If you bought a fake plastic tree some years ago to economise, shame on you: you may as well just cancel Christmas and be done with it. A real tree will set you back €50.

5. Decorations

Working on the assumption that you're not planning to bedeck your house with enough festive illumination to put a small Las Vegas casino to shame, you should get away with spending less than €50, including your lights – presuming that you're not starting completely from scratch. The cost of your decorations does very much depend on where you buy them, though. You can pay close to €50 for a single, very tasteful bauble in Brown Thomas, or for the same amount you could buy enough cheap decorations in Penney's to adorn both your tree and your neighbour's. We'd recommend the latter option. Fairly ordinary Christmas lights will cost another €30.

6. Presents

While the Deloitte study found that the average spend on children was €121 – twice the European average – parents whom PriceWatch spoke to spend considerably more. One father spent €400 on presents for his two children, aged six and one, and another reckons there'll be little change out of €400 for each child. It's not hard to see why: a 4-gigabyte iPod Nano costs €209, while game consoles and phones don't cost much less. When clothes, books and other bits and pieces are factored in, the price of presents rises significantly. For our imaginary family of five, we've allowed €250 per child and €100 per adult, taking the total present spend (not including friends and relatives, who are getting nothing this year) to €950.

7. Santa Claus

No Christmas is complete without a visit to Santa Claus, hidden away at the back of some packed shopping centre. You'd perhaps want to allow €15 per child, a total of €45. Then there's the ice-skating (€50 for our fictional family) and a pantomime (another €70, not including treats), which takes the total cost of Christmassy outings to €165.

8. Christmas cards and postage

While PriceWatch neither sends nor receives many cards, other people are more organised (and more popular). The downside is that, if you're sending forty cards, which will cost you at least €20, you'll need to spend another €0.55 per card on stamps. Suddenly that's another €40 gone.

9. New clothes

If you have any money left after all the present-buying, you might like to buy yourself a new shirt or frock to bedazzle your colleagues while you dance ironically to Nik Kershaw tunes at the Christmas party. Set aside €100 each for these. Embarrassment on the morning after comes free. Children might also be in the market for new clothes – both to sleep in on Christmas Eve and to wear to church services or to the neighbours' the following morning. Another €350 has been spent.

10. Transport

If you want to visit relatives either down the country or in the city, you'll need to get there. A return trip cross-country from Dublin to Galway will cost you about €50 in petrol; this doesn't include a stop in Harry's of Kinnegad. If you're going to take a train, an adult ticket costs €40.50, while children's tickets will set you back €20.50, taking the total public transport cost for the return trip to Galway to more than €140.

11. Power

The savage increases in energy costs announced recently were made slightly less savage soon afterwards thanks to the Energy Regulator rescinding its earlier decision to raise the price of household gas by 34 percent and the price of electricity by 20 percent. Even with the reduced increases, the average monthly gas bill is well in excess of €100, while the monthly electricity bill is currently around €60. Assuming that more gas is spent cooking and heating over the festive period and that more oil is burned keeping the Santa on your roof illuminated, let's allow

€50 for Christmas-related energy costs.

12. Charity

Whether it is to assuage the guilt of spending so much on your own family or the result of high-profile marketing campaigns, donations to charities rise significantly at Christmas. The charities certainly need it. In 2007, the St Vincent de Paul Society (SVP) spent €41 million to help families in need. You might expect to give another €100 to charity in the form of Christmas cards, direct donations and contributions to flag days and carol services.

So my total household spend for what looks like a fairly standard Irish Christmas is an eye-wateringly expensive €2,590 – and the new year has yet to be factored in.

One way to save money on Christmas

Shop early – very, very early. This is going to sound ridiculous, but if you do want to cut down on the cost of Christmas, one thing to consider is doing much of your Christmas shopping immediately after, and not just before, Christmas. Christmas lights which sell for €40 a time can be bought for a tenner in the first week in January. The same is true for all those pretty baubles which, post-Christmas, cost a quarter of the price they did pre-Christmas. I'm not suggesting that you buy your turkey and plum pudding in February, but if there are costs that are commonly associated with your Christmas every year, it is worth buying these things out of season, when they are much cheaper, and sticking them in the attic until the time comes.

Shop in the sales

There's nothing more annoying than paying full price for something only to see it marked 30 percent off in the sales a couple of weeks later. In this world we live in, a sale in some shop is never far away, so if you can just be a little patient, you can make substantial savings. And I'm not suggesting you go shopping on day one of a sale, or queue like an eejit overnight or anything . . . .

Don't spend a lot on the Lotto

Of course it's enticing when the jackpot rolls over and over again and reaches €10 or 12 million, but don't let the advertising and the hype sucker you into buying more than one or two tickets. Your chances of winning the Lotto are around 8 million to one, and they don't improve significantly if you buy ten tickets or one. So save yourself the

money and only buy the one – if you really have to.

Pay for things in one go rather than in instalments by direct debit

If not this year, then next. There is only one reason why that smiling, helpful chap in your local electrical store is asking you if you want an extended warranty, and it's not for your benefit.

Total savings this month: €200

A final word

As I said at the outset, this book was not supposed to offer you a crash course in accountancy. It was not supposed to be filled with incomprehensible tables filled with figures which made your eyes glaze over. The idea has been to show you the importance of thinking a little bit more about where your money is going, and how, by making a few small changes, you can save yourself a fortune.

If you've followed all, or even some, of the tips in this book, made a few sandwiches and a few phone calls (using Skype, maybe) to your banks and credit-card companies and carried out an audit of your insurance products, you should have as much as €3,000, which is enough to get you and someone else a couple of weeks in a very plush hotel anywhere in Europe – as long, of course, as you don't plan to go in high season. Even if you've adopted only a handful of the ideas, you should still find yourself with an extra €500 at the end of the year – money which is better off in your pocket than in anyone else's (except, maybe, mine).

Over to you

Here's a small sample of money-saving tips from listeners to *The Ray Darcy Show* on Today FM and readers of the Pricewatch blog on ireland.com.

If people ask for generic (non-branded) versions of medicines, they can save loads. This applies to over-the-counter (OTC) as well as prescription medicines. For example, a twenty-four pack of non-branded paracetamol (500mg) costs €2, while a twenty-four pack of Panadol costs €2.85. A pack of twenty Motilium costs €9.49, while the same sized packet of Domerid (generic) is €7.49. And because these are medicinal drugs, there is no difference between the branded and generic products in terms of their active ingredients, or when it comes to their quality and efficacy. Watch out for how the doctor has written the prescription, though, so that you aren't given the wrong thing by the pharmacist!
Ultan Molloy, pharmacist

Many people never even try and negotiate a better deal with their car or house insurers. It certainly pays to shop around, but even if you want to stay with your present insurers, do a bit of quick Internet research and get a quote or two from other providers. Then ring your insurance company and say that their quote is not competitive. You will usually find that they will lop anything up to a hundred euro off your premium without much quibble. Of course, the quote you obtained from other sources may not be for as much cover as you presently have, but even the hint that you might be changing insurers usually results in an instant discount on the premium or an upgrade of the cover being offered. Try it, it works!

James McClean

Ask for a discount - whether you're buying a house or a new car (or a horse). If you don't ask, you won't get.

Sarah

Here's a way to save on Ryanair bookings (when you need to check bags in). When booking flights online with Ryanair for family or group holidays, book all the family (or group) on one free web check-in booking (with priority boarding), and book yourself on a separate booking, with airport check-in, to check the necessary bags in (up to three per person). You will avoid paying individual airport check-in charges (€8) and priority boarding charges (€8) for each individual member of the group. One of them can then save you a preferred seat on the plane as they will be near the top of the queue whereas you will be towards the back of it. The bigger the group, the better the saving.

Barry O'Neill

(Author's note: If the three bags you're carrying weigh more than 15 kg, you'll be hit with excess-baggage charges, which will almost certainly wipe out any savings and could even end up costing you money.)

If you're buying a new car and it's close to the end of the month, wait until the start of the next month to take it out of the garage, otherwise you'll end up paying for a month's tax, and probably only get a few days' driving for it. I know a lad who took his new car out on the 31st of January and had to pay tax for all of January! Not good!

Paul Newell

We are a family of two adults and two children trying to book a family holiday for a week at Easter. We found that there were significant savings to be made in flying out of Belfast compared with leaving from the Republic; this was due to the fact that the schools are on holidays down here and not up there. We have seen examples of identical holiday packages leaving from Belfast and Dublin with the same operator costing as much as €1,200 less in Belfast after converting money. The holiday we booked was €700 cheaper.

Paul Bohan

A lot of people on variable or tracker mortgages could be paying too much interest. Interest on mortgages is calculated on a loan-to-value (LTV) basis. People who bought their houses two to three years ago were set a particular interest rate (e.g. 3 percent) and may now be on a much higher rate because the introductory offer has expired and they are paying an interest rate of maybe 5.25 percent (almost twice what they had been paying before). That interest rate is determined by the LTV value, which does not take the increase in value of the house into account. Get a revaluation of the house from the bank or auctioneer, present it to your lender, and you may get a lower interest rate (maybe as low as 4.9 percent), which will save you a few quid every month. And you could ring the mortgage department to see what value your house has to be valued at to drop the interest rate on your mortgage.

Lisa Egan

Compare mortgage offerings using the fundamental numbers (normally APR). Ignore things like two-year discounted rates, 'free' home insurance and other gimmicks: these things do not add up to much over the lifetime of your mortgage, and banks will claw them back down the line.

S. Mulcahy

Even if you're using a broker, do your own analysis on the Web first: an hour will give you summary rates for all the main providers. Don't hesitate to use these as a stick to motivate your broker. They can normally negotiate slightly better rates if encouraged. If using a broker, make sure you know how they get paid, and bear that in mind when reviewing their recommendations.

S. Mulcahy

The best tip I heard was for neighbours to share a wheelie bin. Instead of forking out two lots of €300 in bin charges a year (on top of the €5-a-time emptying tag), you just go halves. Obviously you'd need to get on well with your neighbour and both be committed to recycling a lot of waste, but these are only small hurdles.

Paul

When filling up with petrol, fill up when it's cold, as the petrol is denser at colder temperatures, and you get more for your money. You'd be surprised at how many more miles you can get for the same amount of money. This advice comes via Richard Hammond on *Top Gear*.

Patrick Kinsella, Carlow

Babies are expensive. I know this might not sound like much, but people spend a fortune on baby wipes and other products. What I do is tear each wipe in half, because they are way too big, and a half is enough to be using at a time. They last me much longer.

Mia

Don't be fooled into buying either pre-packaged fruit salads or bagged salad leaves. They cost about three times the price and aren't as good for you. Buy all the ingredients and do the chopping yourself. It's more fun that way too.

Paula

Keep an active change jar going in your house at all times. Every time you come home with a pocket full of shrapnel, just dump it into the jar. You'll be amazed how quickly the money mounts up.

Karl

Most people drink coffee in the morning on work days. I drink Americanos. The cheapest one I have found is €2. My co-workers drink lattes that are as much as €2.50 each! Now, the best bag of ground coffee at Starbucks is €7, and you can get approximately twenty-five cups of coffee out of it. You can buy yourself a cafetière or a mug with a coffee filter attached to it. Of course, you'd make the best savings by quitting your coffee habit and depositing €2 a day in a jar. You'll end up with a nice sum at the end of the year.

Juan Carlos Cordovez

I find that not going shopping when I don't need to really helps when it comes to saving money. I could have shopped for Ireland, but now I find I am not that bothered about it, so I don't even go looking. I think this is an age thing, as after about twenty-five years' shopping, I realised that I have everything I need already.

Belinda O'Dea

Shop locally. Get to know your butcher, fishmonger and greengrocer. You'll get the best advice on produce, the freshest food and the best value, and you'll be supporting your community – unless you're buying strawberries in December, which are perhaps not quite so local.

Sorcha

Don't buy the two-for-one pork fillets or eight discounted chicken breasts unless you're going to eat them or freeze them before the use-by date. Ditto with fruit and veg on special offer. However, do make a comprehensive shopping list, and do a big shop. Plan your meals; don't just buy whatever takes your fancy. In general, look at supermarket items to make sure they are not short-dated. Buy the bread or milk with the longest shelf life: you're more likely to use it all. Lastly, use up leftovers, and make soup, pasta sauces, omelettes, etc.

Sarah Sharkey

As *Viz* magazine once said: 'Don't waste money on expensive iPods, just think of your favourite song and hum it for free.'

Killian

Supermarkets are currently selling expensive tumble-drying balls, which come in a two-pack for €10 to €14. These balls claim to cut your tumble-drying costs by up to 60 percent. Well, instead of buying these balls, I have found that tennis balls work just as well. You'll pick these up for a euro or two, so in fact you are making a double saving!

S. Clarke

You almost need to take out a loan to go to the cinema these days. Why not go to the early-bird showing, which is usually before 1 PM . In Mahon Point, Cork, for example, it costs around €5 before 1 PM to go and see the same film you'd see a few hours later for €9.50: a saving of €4.50. You might as well make a day of it with your family or friends and go for a meal afterwards. Spend the saving on a glass of wine if you want!

Emma Davies

Useful contacts

Financial Regulator
Dame Street, Dublin 2
1890 777 777
itsyourmoney.ie

Commission for Communication Regulation (COMREG)
Abbey Court, Irish Life Centre,
Lower Abbey Street, Dublin 1
Tel. 01 804 9600; Fax 01 804 9680;
e-mail info@comreg.ie
callcosts.ie
comreg.ie

National Consumer Agency
4 Harcourt Road, Dublin 2
1890 432432
www.consumerconnect.ie

The European Consumer Centre
eccdublin.ie

Solicitors
The Law Society, Blackhall Place,
Dublin 7

Independent Adjudicator of the Law Society
26/27 Upper Pembroke Street,
Dublin 2

Pensions
The Office of the Pension Ombudsman
PO Box 9324, 36 Upper Mount
Street, Dublin 2
(01) 647 1650

The Advertising Standards Authority of Ireland
IPC House, 35/39 Shelbourne
Road, Dublin 4
Tel. (01) 660 8766; Fax (01) 660
8113; Email standards@asai.ie
asai.ie

Citizens Information Call Centre

7th Floor, Hume House,
Ballsbridge, Dublin 4

1890 777 121;

information@comhairle.ie
citizensinformation.ie

The Consumer Association of Ireland

43–44 Chelmsford Road,
Ranelagh, Dublin 6

01 479 8600

consumerassociation.ie

STOP WASTING YOUR MONEY

STOP WASTING YOUR MONEY

NOTES

STOP WASTING YOUR MONEY